HARDSHIP AND HOPE - HEBDEN ROYD & TODMORDEN DURING THE FIRST WORLD WAR (1914-1918

First published 2016
Copyright © 2016 Peter Thomas
All rights reserved
The greatest care has been taken to ascertain ownership of copyright
of images featured in this book and where necessary
permission has been sought and obtained.

Published by Peter Thomas
email plkthomas@hotmail.com

In print by the same author -
The Good Ship Calder High and Other Tales from the 1950s.

Produced in Great Britain by
Pennine Printing Services
Barkisland, Halifax, West Yorkshire, England

ISBN 978-0-9535405-4-9

Front Cover left: Wilfred Uttley; a popular young man of promise.
Front Cover right: Wilfred Uttley, one of the three former employees of Thomas Ashworth who had been lost by August 1916.
Back Cover: The solemn funeral cortege of Wilfred Uttley.

Hardship and Hope - Hebden Royd & Todmorden During The First World War (1914-1918

By Peter Thomas

ACKNOWLEDGEMENTS

In the absence of first-hand oral evidence, I have relied heavily on information provided by contemporary issues of the *Hebden Bridge Times* and the *Hebden Bridge and District News*. In this respect I owe a great debt of gratitude to Stuart Gill, who allowed me to use books of cuttings from these publications compiled by his grandfather.

Thanks are also due to the following : -
Frank Woolrych, of Pennine Horizons, who has taken great pains to restore old photographs and other material to publishable form.

Ann Kilby also contributed her time and computer expertise.

Mike Crawford, who has provided help and encouragement.

Steve Wright for giving me access to the diary of his great-grandfather, Ernest Law, a piece of eye-witness evidence which gave an insight into the tragedy of Gallipoli.

John Rhodes, who furnished me with authoritative information concerning local Military Tribunals and conscientious objectors.

Mike Edwards, for going to much trouble to provide me with local casualty statistics.

The following people assisted me in terms of providing information, photographs, artefacts and other material. To them I tender my thanks : - David Blanchard, Russell Dean, Bryan Earnshaw, Stephen Gee, Stuart Greenwood, Wayne Ogden, Peter Robertshaw, Issy Shannon, Keith Stansfield, Alexander Thomas, Luke Thomas, Simeon Thomas, John Uttley, Betty Veevers and
the War Veterans' Association of Australia.

I am grateful also to the staff at Bankfield Museum, Halifax, for allowing me to use material from the Great War Galleries.

Finally a huge thanks to my wife, Louise, for word processing, editing, correcting, photographing, assisting with research and not least, for her unwavering support and enthusiasm from beginning to end of this project.

CONTENTS

Introduction 7

1. Just Another Assassination? 11
2. The War of Words 13
3. Over by Christmas? 17
4. Appeals and Atrocities 23
5. Should I Stay or Should I Go? 27
6. Shoulders to the Wheel 33
7. They Also Serve 39
8. Soldiers' Stories 47
9. Todmorden's Tragedy – Gallipoli 53
10. Conscription 63
11. The Rush to the Back 67
12. Won't Fight; Can't Fight 75
13. King Khaki 83
14. Feeling the Strain 89
15. Keep Right On 97
16. Money, Money, Money 103
17. Help in all Directions 111
18. The Bitter End 117
19. A Time to Reflect 123

HARDSHIP AND HOPE - HEBDEN ROYD & TODMORDEN DURING THE FIRST WORLD WAR (1914-1918)

INTRODUCTION

To begin at the end.... In November 1918 a young soldier lay dying in 2 Western General Hospital, Grange Street, Manchester. His name was Robert Arnold Thomas; his age 21; a private in the Royal Fusiliers. He had been wounded near Albert, in France, on August 5th 1918, and his left leg had been amputated at a Casualty Clearing Station. Later he was transferred to Manchester, and by October it was known that he was critically ill and his family was visiting him. One can imagine those sad railway journeys from a smoke-filled Hebden Bridge to a similarly blighted Manchester on grey late autumn days – a family having to accept that one of its own could not be saved, that his life was slowly ebbing away. On November 16th (five days after the Armistice) Robert died under anaesthetic whilst undergoing an operation to remove pus from the hip joint.

Robert Arnold Thomas – just another soldier, just another war, just another death – a man soon to be forgotten to history. Was this all it had come down to after all the talk of glory and honour? Not quite… Robert's older brother, James, was determined to pay his own small tribute to his younger brother. In common with many Sunday School scholars of the time, James had been presented with a Lord Wharton Bible at St. James' Church, Hebden Bridge, in 1903. In November 1918 he wrote on the flyleaf –

"Robert. Age 21.

My brother died of wounds in hospital in Manchester, Nov. 16th 1918, received in action to the right of Albert, Aug. 5th 1918, in Belgium, during the Great European war, Aug. 4th 1914 to Nov. 11th 1918.

Greater love hath no man
than this,
That he lay down his life
for his friends.
He gave his life that we
might live."

The headstone of Robert Arnold Thomas in the churchyard of St. Thomas à Becket, Heptonstall.
Louise Thomas

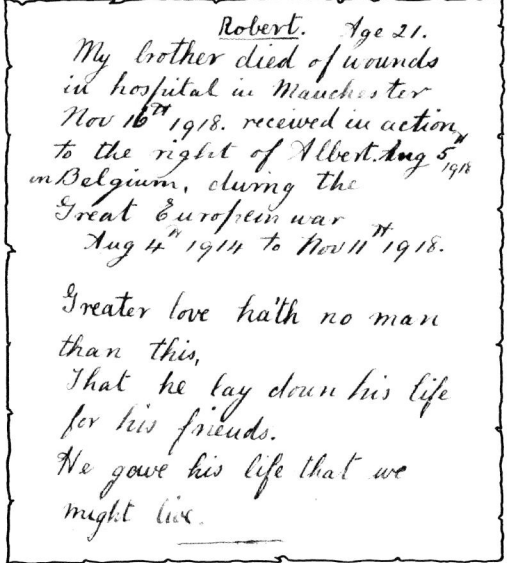

Part of the inscription in the Lord Wharton Bible.

Simple words to express the agony of grief, and where better to put them than within a book which James may well have believed to contain some hope of renewal and reunion.

At some stage, however, this Bible went on its travels, only to resurface many years later. Early in 2013 a gentleman from Huddersfield turned up at the office of Hebden Royd C. of E. Primary School. An avid collector of war related items, he had picked up the Bible in a 'junk' shop in South Yorkshire. Recognising the link with St. James' Church he had come to the school in the hope that the Bible might in some way be restored to its original family. He handed the book over to the School Administrator. James Thomas' Bible had returned home.

The interest aroused by the Bible and its inscription was the genesis of this book. First of all, who were these brothers, James and Robert Thomas? They were the two sons of John Thomas, living with him, their stepmother Annabella, and two sisters at 24 Oak Street, Hebden Bridge. In common with most of the inhabitants of Hebden Bridge, the Thomas family earned its living from the clothing trade. The head of the family, John, was a warehouseman. Prior to his enlistment into the army, Robert had worked for Edward Greenwood & Co. at the nearby Victoria Clothing Works. Again in common with many young men of his time, Robert was a member of the local parish church and Sunday School.

Secondly, how did this very ordinary family, like so many about them, come to get caught up

were serious doubts ever raised locally about the purpose and duration of the conflict?

in the world-wide tragedy that became known as the Great War? What impact did this war have on the town and its Upper Calder Valley neighbours? If the war began with a unity forged by patriotism, did the mounting losses, combined with domestic strains, cause any fractures to appear in the local Home Front? As one weary year of war followed another, with increasing bloodshed, were serious doubts ever raised locally about the purpose and duration of the conflict? These are the kind of questions that this book will attempt to answer.

'Hardship' and 'Hope' are the two key words in the title. Total war meant the involvement of the British people in the conflict on a scale never witnessed before. First of all, a huge army was required. Therefore the first call was the one made to young men to fight for king and country. The hardship on the Home Front lay with their families left behind – sometimes financial hardship, always emotional hardship bound up with the fear of loss. As the war unfolded, a host of other problems presented themselves, with varying degrees of hardship – shortages of food and other consumer goods, resulting in rocketing prices and suspicion of profiteering; fear of aerial attack and the imposition of blackouts and other lighting restrictions; the huge powers invested in the government by the Defence of the Realm Act (1914), giving it the right to interfere in all

work harder, waste less, save more

walks of life, including censorship of the press, in the name of national security; the pressures imposed by the recruiting campaign followed by the introduction of conscription in 1916. Finally, throughout the war, people faced the constant urgings of the government to work harder, waste less, save more and invest in war bonds. Otherwise the war might be lost and the sacrifice of life be in vain.

Where was the hope in all this? In the long term it lay in the conviction that this was a just war and in accepting the government's arguments that sacrifices would not be in vain and that a better world would emerge from it all. Day by day, however, the hope of people living through these grim days was a more modest one, though no less important, that the man or men in their family would survive. That is not to say that families were insensitive to the losses of others. Hebden Bridge gets its fair share of media coverage nowadays, and is sometimes labelled, 'a tightly knit community.' This is a lazy cliché for what is, in reality, a set of disparate groups who rub along reasonably well together. The Hebden Bridge of 1914-18 really was a tightly knit community in which many people had deep local roots. Living 'cheek by jowl' in the tightly packed terraces, they worked together in the local mills and often sat together in churches and chapels.

Therefore, as the casualties mounted year by year, and names and photographs appeared in the local press, it is likely that most people knew or knew of the fallen men. The astonishing number of Greenwoods and Sutcliffes in the casualty lists, belonging to all

> *Todmorden has a special relationship to the disastrous Gallipoli Campaign of 1915*

social levels, indicates strongly forged links between old Calder Valley families. Hence the resonance of the losses would have reverberated more strongly in Hebden Bridge and its neighbouring communities than would likely be the case today.

Speaking of neighbouring communities brings up the question of the geographical scope of this book. The focus is Hebden Bridge, but events and people from Luddenden Foot to Todmorden, including the hill top villages, are featured. Todmorden receives frequent mentions, particularly in relation to the Centre Vale Military Hospital established there. However, Todmorden has a special relationship to the disastrous Gallipoli Campaign of 1915 and a whole chapter is devoted to this. The germ of this book was an interest inspired by an inscription found in a Bible. It has grown into a tribute to the people of the Upper Calder Valley who stoically endured a massive conflict in which demands for sacrifice were met at every level, including the ultimate one. And to the men of this district who made the supreme sacrifice, there could be no more fitting tribute than the one inscribed on the Centre Vale Memorial in Todmorden. It was in honour of the men of Todmorden, but it could well have applied to all the local men who, "at the call of King and Country, and in defence of their Native Land, left all that was dear to them, endured hardship, faced danger, and finally passed out of the sight of Man by the path of Duty and Self-sacrifice, giving up their own lives that others might live in Freedom."

CHAPTER 1 – JUST ANOTHER ASSASSINATION?

On June 28th 1914 two shots rang out on the streets of Sarajevo, the capital of Bosnia, two shots that perhaps ultimately took the lives of around ten million people. The immediate impact was the deaths of Archduke Franz Ferdinand, heir to the throne of Austria-Hungary, and his wife Sophie. They had been paying a state visit to Bosnia, a part of the sprawling Austro-Hungarian Empire, but when their car stalled in the narrow streets of Sarajevo, the incident provided an all too tempting target for Gavrilo Princip, a Bosnian nationalist and a member of the improbably named Black Hand Gang. The pre-arranged assassination plot seemed to have been bungled but fate had given Princip an unexpected opportunity. He stepped onto the running board and fired two shots into the open-topped vehicle. Sophie died immediately; her husband a few minutes later.

The news agencies spread the story throughout the world and on July 3rd it made its appearance in a short couple of paragraphs in the *Hebden Bridge Times*. Entitled 'Assassination of Royalties,' an odd little mistake had entered the piece. The male victim was named as Archduke Francis Joseph rather than Archduke Franz Ferdinand. The former was the existing Emperor of Austria - Hungary, not the heir to the throne. The article then went on to describe the near lynching of the assassin, Gavrilo Princip, by the infuriated crowd incensed by the, "dastardly outrage." Perhaps the mistake was indicative of the somewhat casual approach to the story. The assassinations were sensational and horrible enough, but not uncommon in the turbulent politics of the Balkans in the early twentieth century which had built up some insensitivity in Western Europe to turmoil in this area. Perhaps it was ….. just another assassination.

It is doubtful if the people of the Upper Calder Valley took much notice of the event. They had more pressing concerns. The holidays were imminent and no doubt the announcement in the *Hebden Bridge Times* by the Lancashire and Yorkshire and Great Northern Railway of its 'Express Holiday Excursions' to various seaside destinations held at least as much interest as Balkan affairs. Then again the Mytholmroyd Charity Demonstration and Fete was due to take place on Saturday July 11th, with the irresistible promise of 'Knockabout Trick Cyclists,' a 'Burmese Magician,' the 'Eccentric Juggler,' a Punch and Judy show, a drill competition for local Boys' Brigades and Boy Scouts, and the grand climax of fireworks at dusk.

> **RAILWAY NOTICES.**
>
> LANCASHIRE & YORKSHIRE AND GREAT NORTHERN RAILWAYS.
>
> ## Express Holiday Excursions
>
> FROM EASTWOOD, HEBDEN BRIDGE, MYTHOLMROYD, LUDDENDEN FOOT AND SOWERBY BRIDGE.
>
> TO WEST OF ENGLAND (PLYMOUTH, ILFRACOMBE, EXETER, BARNSTAPLE, etc.), each Friday, and to SOUTH OF ENGLAND (BRIGHTON, BOURNEMOUTH, EASTBOURNE, HASTINGS, etc.), each Friday and July 6th and 20th, for 8 or 15 days.
> To CAMBRIDGE, GRANTHAM, HITCHIN, LETCHWORTH, NEWARK, SANDY, &c., on JULY 6th and 20th, for 2 or 5 days.
> To LONDON (KING'S CROSS) on July 6th and 20th, for 2, 5 or 8 days, and July 4th for 2, 3 or 5 days, and 11th for 2, 3 or 5 days, 13th for 2, 5 or 8 days, 18th for 3, 5, or 8 days, 25th for 3, 6 or 8 days, 27th for 2, 5 or 8 days.
> For full particulars see Bills at Stations.
> By Order.

People's minds were on the imminent summer holidays, not the Balkans.

As always the weather was a constant source of conversation, especially with the holidays looming up. In contrast to the nostalgic image of the golden and glorious summers of those pre-war days, the weather in June had been wet

---
a lightning strike had rendered a young man blind in his own kitchen

---

and cold. Worse, violent thunderstorms had struck this and other parts of the country the previous week. The centre of Bradford had been flooded in a deluge of rain. In Smallbridge in Lancashire a haymaker had been killed by lightning. In Sowerby Bridge a lightning strike had rendered a young man blind in his own kitchen. Would storm clouds return to ruin the holidays? They were certainly gathering elsewhere.

Although the Sarajevo assassinations had disappeared from the headlines, behind the scenes the diplomatic ripples were spreading across Europe and steadily gathering strength. The Austro-Hungarian government had no doubt that Serbia, in its attempts to assist its fellow Slavs in Bosnia to escape from Germanic rule, was behind the assassinations. Nevertheless, swift action would have been unwise as Russia was poised to help its fellow Slav 'brother' Serbia. Not until Austria-Hungary had been given assurances of assistance from Germany could she move. Therefore it was not until July 25th 1914 that Austria-Hungary declared war on Serbia.

What could be called the domino effect then ensued. Deciding on a pre-emptive strike, Germany declared war on Russia on August 1st and on France (Russia's ally) on August 3rd. When Germany put into operation its Schlieffen Plan and poured troops into neutral Belgium in order to strike a hammer blow at France, the British government decided to stand firm. Britain had been one of the guarantors of Belgian neutrality in a treaty of

> *"The lamps are going out across Europe."*

1839 and the Foreign Secretary, Sir Edward Grey, issued an ultimatum to the German government that unless it agreed to evacuate its troops from Belgium by 11 p.m., August 4th, Britain would declare war on Germany. The story goes that Grey stood listening to the chimes of Big Ben at 11 p.m. on that fateful evening and said sadly, "The lamps are going out across Europe." Indeed the continent which prided itself on possessing the most advanced civilisation in the world was about to be plunged into darkness for over four years. The false calm after Sarajevo had ended in a rush and suddenly the British people found themselves at war.

CHAPTER 2 – THE WAR OF WORDS

In London the outbreak of war was greeted with huge expressions of patriotism. Even before the official announcement on August 4th, crowds milled around central London, marching and singing. Union flags and French tricolours could be seen everywhere. No doubt it was exciting to be at the centre of events and people were swept along with the tide. The most prominent figure to speak out against the war was Keir Hardie, the veteran former leader of the Labour Party, but the small anti-war demonstration he addressed in Trafalgar Square seemed to strike a false note amidst the general rejoicing.

There was a more subdued response away from the big cities. An editorial in the *Halifax Evening Courier* on August 3rd 1914, on the very eve of war, lamented the fact that at least some of the press was playing on public opinion in order to push it into a pro-war stance. Both this newspaper and the *Hebden Bridge Times* doubted whether either side would be able to obtain a quick and decisive victory. Also a more sober stance was adopted by the Neutrality League, the local branch of which took out a full page advertisement in the *Courier* urging people to join the campaign to keep out of the war. Nevertheless once horns had been locked, the local press felt it its duty to follow the official patriotic line, and in many ways it had little option as the government controlled Press Bureau operated tight censorship. War journalists were kept strictly in the rear and war news was filtered to the press via the Press Bureau

There is no doubt then that the editorial in the *Hebden Bridge Times* of August 7th 1914 reflected the official line. Local people needed to be convinced that the war was more than just about the violations of Belgium's neutrality. Kaiser Wilhelm II, Emperor of Germany, had dismissed the guarantee of neutrality as merely a 'scrap of paper.' To most British people, perhaps the concept of honour in terms of Britain fighting to defend Belgium's neutrality was important but a little abstract. There

Not everyone was caught up in war fever.

needed to be more to it than this. These deeper reasons for war were expressed in the headline for the editorial – 'TEUTONIC AMBITION AIMING AT BRITAIN.' The editorial laid the blame for the war squarely on Germany's plate. "All so called talks have been merely a pretence," under the cover of which, "Germany has been secretly mobilising." The editorial than went on to reveal Germany's real aim which was to seize the Channel ports, cut off the route to the Empire along with British imports, and thus to isolate and starve Britain into surrender whilst Germany took over the domination of Europe.

With the *Hebden Bridge Times* laying out such an uncompromising message, it did not take long for local patriotism to emerge. The issue of September 9th 1914 published two local poems. One was from W.W. Graham of High Greenwood, Heptonstall, and was entitled

Your King and Your Country Need You. This rallying call was accompanied by a passionate but anonymous piece entitled *The Kaiser and God*. A few lines encapsulate its flavour:-

> "Kaiser when you kneel in prayer
> Look upon your hands, and there
> Let that deep and awful stain
> From the blood of children slain
> Burn your very soul with shame."

With such a mood abroad, it was perhaps unwise that the Independent Labour Party at this point proposed to hold a protest meeting in Fielden Square, Todmorden. The theme of the meeting, which was also to be attended by, "local reverend gentlemen," was to be 'War Against War.' However, the I.L.P. was warned that there would almost certainly be trouble if the meeting was held outdoors and the group quietly adjourned to the Co-operative Hall where there was, "a small gathering."

It may seem strange that a war with Germany was so readily accepted by the British people. Here were two nations with strong racial and economic links and whose monarchs, George V and Kaiser Wilhelm II were cousins. The latter, however, was unstable and unpredictable. His insistence on building up a battle fleet to match Britain's (with no empire to speak of to protect) caused mistrust and fear in Britain, as did his very vocal support for the Boers during the Boer War of 1899 to 1902. The main threat to Britain had once seemed to be France, but now the focus had switched to Germany. Books such as *The Riddle of the Sands* by Erskine Childers, warned of an imminent German threat, and pre-war boys' comics, such as *The Magnet*, often featured German invasion stories.

On top of all this, no sooner had war broken out than stories of German spies began feverishly to circulate. An editorial in the *Hebden Bridge Times* for August 14th 1914 warned about, "military desperadoes disguised as civilians", who had been dispatched to Britain from Germany before the war with the aim of sabotage and spying. The public was warned to be on the alert. All tunnels on the Lancashire and Yorkshire Railway were being guarded day and night. Even four ordnance survey map surveyors were arrested and briefly detained after being found 'lurking' near a reservoir at Mount Tabor. *The Hebden Bridge Times* for October 23rd 1914 roundly condemned Germany as being, "a nation of spies," spying being, "second nature to them." Seemingly German spies had been swarming into Belgium, Luxembourg, France and England for many years. A book on this subject was snapped up by the public, selling 40,000 copies in one week in 1915. Apparently the term 'German measles' was now intolerable and it was replaced by the name 'Belgian flush.'

> *George V and Kaiser Wilhelm II were cousins. The latter, however, was unstable and unpredictable*

The German "Banned."

Anti-German feeling was rife.

Courtesy of Bankfield Museum

In this fevered atmosphere anti-German feeling was intense. In their book *All Quiet on the Home Front*, Richard van Emden and Steve Humphries suggest that Germans living in England were at the receiving end of much worse treatment than that meted out in World War Two. Of the 53,000 Germans living in Britain in 1914, only 22,000 were left by the end of the war. Many were put in internment camps and deported at the end of the war, even those married to British women with British born children. Stoked up by the jingoistic press, hatred sometimes spilled over into violence, as witnessed in Birmingham, for example, with attacks on German owned shops and their proprietors.

This undoubtedly put William Dehner, a pork butcher in Hebden Bridge, into a difficult if not dangerous position. William had left his home town of Künzelsau, in the Black Forest region of Germany, around 1880/1881. A wheelwright by trade and with the equivalent of £11 in his pocket, his intention was to seek a better life by emigrating to the U.S.A. Things didn't quite work out that way and William ended up as an apprentice butcher in the Little Germany part of Bradford where he met and married a fellow German national, Kate Strecker in 1884. By 1901 William and Kate were living in Hebden Bridge where William had set himself up as a pork butcher with premises in Market Street and Bridge Gate. By the outbreak of war William was a naturalised Englishman, a respected local citizen and councillor with six children, three boys and three girls. Nevertheless William and his wife must have felt some alarm at the anti-German mood of the nation, and a local story had it that the owner of some kennels up Heptonstall Road had arrived one morning to find his six dachshunds kicked to death.

It was therefore very early in the war that William Dehner made a public statement of his allegiance. At a meeting of the local council at Hebden Bridge in mid-August 1914, Councillor Dehner made a patriotic speech, stating that he was totally loyal to his adopted country. Furthermore, he had sent his son to,

William Dehner outside his pork butcher's shop.

Courtesy of Russell Dean

"volunteer for service under the British flag," and that if need be, he himself would fight. The dangers to people such as him were very real. In May 1915 the Cunard passenger liner, *Lusitania*, was torpedoed and sunk off the coast of Ireland with a loss of 1198 civilians. This further increased anti-German feeling, and one week later William Dehner was one of a group of West Yorkshire naturalised Germans, largely businessmen, who signed a protest against German outrages at Bradford Town Hall. They cited, as examples, the sinking of the *Lusitania* and the shocking behaviour of the German army in Belgium and France. The signatories wanted to place on record their, "horror and indignation."

William was as good as his word in having declared, in August 1914, that his family would fight for the flag. His eldest son, Albert, was listed in the *Hebden Bridge Times* for August 7th 1914 as one of twenty local men who had already departed for war service, and he was reported as having been wounded in August 1916. William's second son, John Frederick, saw action in Mesopotamia. However, it was William Dehner's eldest daughter, Rose, who made the greatest sacrifice. Her husband, John Most, a member of the family business, enlisted in the Labour Corps in July 1916. Sadly he contracted meningitis whilst serving in France, dying in hospital in Dieppe on May 24th 1917. *The Hebden Bridge Times* published a sympathetic obituary and stressed that, "other members of the family are patriotically serving this country."

In spite of all this, at some stage in the war someone felt aggrieved enough to throw a brick through the window of William Dehner's pork butcher's shop. It is difficult to know whether this was the result of some latent anti-German animosity or, more likely, part of a dispute over a pig killing at a stage in the war when shortages and rationing were imposing some hardship on local people. It was probably the memory of incidents such as this, along with a wish to integrate more fully into British society, which caused William's sons to change their surname from 'Dehner' to 'Dean' after the war. The son of John Frederick was Russell Dean, a highly successful local businessman, who has fond memories of his grandfather (still William *Dehner*) living in retirement for many years at Wheat Ing, highly respected in the locality and much loved by his family. William died in 1949 at the age of 85.

William Dehner in his old age.

Courtesy of Russell Dean

CHAPTER 3 – OVER BY CHRISTMAS?

Even though the three wars prior to 1914 between major European powers – those fought in the 1860s by Prussia against Denmark, Austria-Hungary and France - had lasted a matter of months, or even weeks, it is doubtful if anyone really in the know ever seriously uttered the words, "Over by Christmas". Behind the propaganda war of words lurked realities that sober judges were well aware of. At the very outset of war, both the *Halifax Evening Courier* and the *Hebden Bridge Times* expressed doubt as to whether a conflict between well-matched and highly industrialised nations could quickly be resolved. Early in August 1914 the local councils met in a conference hosted by the Chairman of the Hebden Bridge Urban District Council, Councillor A. Sutcliffe. His gloomy forecast predicted severe disruption to world trade resulting in distress and unemployment for Hebden Bridge. He appealed to people to, "husband their resources," and not spend money on luxuries.

If the outbreak of war had been greeted by wild enthusiasm by some in London, a very different attitude was expressed from the pulpit at Birchcliffe, Hebden Bridge, by the Reverend J.H.J. Plumbridge, on August 9th 1914. He gave a graphic warning of what modern war could entail – "cities devastated; men killed and wounded in tens of thousands." Not only this, he put the blame squarely on the shoulders of two or three heads of state and stated that never again must the power, "to plunge a continent into all the horrors of war rest in such irresponsible hands as these." Even so, the Reverend Plumbridge laid no blame on Britain, insisting that the country was engaged in a chivalrous defence of a smaller state being trampled on by militarism. These latter sentiments were shared by sermons given in churches at Mytholmroyd and Heptonstall. For those who preferred a more upbeat approach, the programme for the Royal Electric Theatre, Hebden Bridge, for August 28th 1914, included a 'Special War Film.' Some of the stirring scenes promised were – 'Off to the Front,' 'Tommy Atkins,' 'Our Allies – Vive la France' and 'The Enemy – the Germans and Austrians.' The whole patriotic programme concluded with a rendition of 'God Save the King.'

The epitome of the 'Bulldog Spirit.

The apocalyptic vision of what war could mean as stated by the Reverend Plumbridge was not reflected in the correspondence columns of the *Hebden Bridge Times*. The reality of war for many was a fear of shortages and high prices. In spite of government reassurances about prices, a letter to the newspaper expressed anxiety about the price of milk. This was an early shot in a war which rumbled on beneath the surface on the Home Front for the duration of the war, fuelled by a suspicion that monopolists and profiteers were making mountains of money out of the war whilst others were sacrificing their lives. In early 1915 delegates to a meeting of the Todmorden and District Trades and Labour Council, held at the Weavers' Institute, gave full vent to their fury at this issue. It was claimed that the price of milk locally had gone up by 17% since the start of the war; that wheat to local millers, although it had been in stock since August 1914, had increased in price from 25 shillings to £3 per load. The Chairman of the meeting Mr T.A. Taylor, claimed that, "Whilst the workers are making sacrifices to the extent of the last drop of their blood, there is a commercial class of people, every member of which should be clapped in gaol." Others railed against the, "insatiable greed and rapacity of a few private monopolists," whilst Mr Ben Thomas stated that the local Labour Party could well declare itself antagonistic to recruiting if the government failed to address this issue. Nevertheless, a resolution of the meeting for the government to take control of both food supplies and prices fell, for the moment, on deaf ears.

Others railed against the, "insatiable greed and rapacity of a few private monopolists"

The reality of war for some, however, seemed to revolve around the vexed problem of alcohol. By November 1914 a long debate was in progress in the correspondence columns of the *Hebden Bridge Times* on the issue of public houses and the war. In one corner stood Mr Ben Wilde, who not only approved of a moderate alcohol issue to soldiers, but at the same time took furious swipes at Mr Sugden Lund, his opponent in the other corner. Mr Lund was a 'Rechabite Missioner,' advocating teetotalism for everyone, but especially pinpointing the demoralising effect of strong drink on soldiers. The battle of words raged on, with the brewers naturally pitching in on the side of Mr Wilde. A letter from Mr W.T. Dupree, representing the brewers, vehemently opposed Lloyd George's War Tax on beer, asserting that it would put an end to, "honest beer drinking," and turn the working classes to spirits.

Clearly the editor of the *Hebden Bridge Times* felt that his column space could be devoted to more weighty matters and on December 11th 1914 he inserted a note stating that, "this controversy must now close." For some reason he was unable to bring about closure and the dispute between Mr Wilde and Mr Lund rumbled on in the letters column. Some people had heard quite enough of the exchanges between Mr Wilde and Mr Lund. A letter signed 'Fed-up' appeared in the *Hebden Bridge Times* on January 29th 1915, pleading for no more arguments in the press between the Rechabites and the pro-drink lobby. It was to no avail. The barbs were still flying between the principal opponents in the very next issue. It was seemingly a war without end!

Alcohol was an issue of much interest, for the temperance movement was in full cry during the early years of the twentieth century, apportioning much blame to the 'demon drink' for working class poverty and domestic violence. On January 23rd 1915 the annual general meeting of the Hebden Bridge branch of the Women's Temperance Association took place at Salem Sunday School. The President, Mrs Eardley, commended the government for shortening public house opening hours, but demanded that strong drink should be totally prohibited during the war and particularly stressed the unwiseness of giving alcohol to soldiers.

One result of the outbreak of war in August 1914 was possibly quite unexpected, but it very quickly became a reality for the locality, this being the demand for horses to be provided for military purposes. The Great War was only in part a mechanical conflict. Horses in large numbers were needed for transport purposes, and as it was intended to rapidly increase the army, this need was urgent. Therefore it was a large and curious crowd which assembled outside the *White Lion* in Hebden Bridge, on Monday August 10th, to see horses purchased for war. Draught horses for artillery and heavy wagon work were what the military was seeking, and of the horses brought in, nine were purchased, "at good market prices."

This seems to have been a voluntary agreement, but on Tuesday more high-handed methods were used. Officials passing through the district in motor cars stopped several carters and commandeered their horses. Twelve were taken and branded for military service. One of the 'victims' was Matthew Sheard, coal merchant and head of a business that has survived until the present day. Doubtless this procedure took place on several occasions and must have had some effect on local economic life. However there was more to horses than simply economic units. Their emotional pull was expressed in a quote from the *Hebden Bridge Times* which curiously pre-figured the theme of Michael Morpurgo's modern work, *War Horse*. "It was a pathetic scene to see the cream of the horses of the district called on for war purposes."

Of course, the greatest reality of all was not the spectre of shortages and high prices, nor the fear of demon drink, not even the loss of horses, but the steady leakage of men from the district. Even before the official declaration of war, mobilisation orders had been received in Hebden Bridge by 9 p.m. on Tuesday, August 4th 1914. By 11 p.m. 40 to 50 territorials had mustered, and they joined with others from lower down the valley to march off to the Duke of Wellington's regimental depot, Halifax. The Todmorden territorials, linked to the Lancashire Fusiliers, marched off in a different direction, towards Rochdale on August 7th, accompanied part of the way by a brass band.

Territorials, often known as 'part-time soldiers,' were men who did ordinary civilian

These were the kind of heavy draught horses that the military had its eye on.

Courtesy of Pennine Horizons

jobs but enhanced their income by becoming linked to a local regiment and doing some weekly military training. They were departing now to receive more training at military camps, and although the territorial force was principally aimed at home defence, these 'part-timers' were now being given the opportunity to become 'full-timers' and serve overseas.

However, there were men from Hebden Bridge and district who were thrust straight into the conflict. These were reservists, men who had already served seven years in the army as regular soldiers, had left for civilian life, but were paid to be 'on reserve' for a further five years. The *Hebden Bridge Times* for August 7th 1914 printed the following list of local reservists who had left immediately for war service. These were:-

James Weatherhead naval reservist
Albert Gibson   J.W.Greenwood
Tom Greenwood   Vincent O'Connor
J. Holmes   Brearley Hellowell
Owen Bell   T. Fossett
C.J. Green   Arthur Thompson
Percy Scott   W. Oldfield
W. Schofield   T.A. Sutcliffe
J.T. Bellfield   John Starkie

Also listed as joining up were three members of the local yeomanry (volunteer cavalry) units – Walter Moss, Laurence Ashworth and Albert Dehner. R. Fruhe Sutcliffe of Heptonstall, although a territorial, seems to have been called into action immediately, but as a Royal Engineer perhaps his services were needed promptly. On August 14th six stretcher bearers belonging to the Hebden Bridge Corps of the St. John Ambulance Brigade awaited orders to join the British Expeditionary Force (B.E.F.) as part of the Royal Army Medical Corps. Thirty five had volunteered for service at home or abroad.

As these men of the district departed, perhaps some of them felt regret or apprehension, whilst others may have been buoyed up by excitement and optimism. Did any of them feel that it would be over by Christmas? Sadly, for four of these reservists,

that was the case. John Willie Greenwood, aged 30, was a reservist from East Parade, Mytholmroyd, employed at Ratcliffe's blanket mill. Thomas Greenwood, aged 31, was from Goitside, Luddenden. Both of them belonged to the local Duke of Wellington's Regiment and died on August 24th 1914 during the heavy fighting around Mons. Three postmen were numbered amongst this early batch of reservists – Percy Scott, Vincent O'Connor and Brearley Hellowell. Percy Scott, a Wadsworth postman and a private in the King's Own Scottish Borderers, was killed near Ypres on November 22nd 1914. (Brearley Hellowell was to be killed in March 1915.) Private John Thomas Bellfield, aged 28, of King Street, Hebden Bridge, a member of the Yorkshire Regiment, died in late 1914.

Vincent O'Connor; a postman and reservist – immediately called up in August 1914; killed in 1917.

Samuel Heap, aged 32, was another man with local connections who died in the early weeks of the war. Although a resident of Burnley in 1914, he had been brought up in Hebden Bridge, having attended Stubbings School, and his parents still lived at Broughton Street. Sam had spent his entire army career with the Black Watch and died of wounds in a military hospital in France on September 27th 1914. Two more deaths in September were those of James Higgins of Charlestown, serving in the Royal Irish Rifles, and Lance Corporal Arthur Holmes (another 'Duke') of Heptonstall Road, Hebden Bridge.

Britain had a huge role to play at sea in this war, and in this sphere too there were early casualties. On September 22nd 1914 a single German 'U'-boat sank three British light cruisers in the North Sea – *Hogue, Cressy and Aboukir*. All the ships sank quickly and naval reservist William Finnigan, of Milner Royd Luddenden Foot, was one of the men lost on *Hogue*. Perhaps even more tragically, *Aboukir* was a training ship for cadets, and amongst the many young sailors drowned was sixteen year old Herbert Riley of Richmond and Mytholmroyd. The losses however, were not confined to front-line servicemen. Ambulanceman Walter Jackson of Sackville Street, Hebden Bridge, formerly a worker at Ashworth's shuttle shop and a volunteer in the Royal Naval Division, died of pneumonia whilst on duty.

It is difficult to know how wholeheartedly the citizens of the Upper Calder Valley celebrated the Christmas of 1914. Back in August, Councillor A. Sutcliffe of the Hebden Bridge Urban District Council had warned of the shortages that would inevitably accompany a European war, and had emphasized the need for economy and self-sacrifice. But it was clear now that there was a much greater burden to be borne – the sacrifice in human lives – and with no end in sight. If anyone had lightly trotted out the phrase, "Over by Christmas," then the question now was – which Christmas?

CHAPTER 4 – APPEALS AND ATROCITIES

The Secretary of State for War, Lord Kitchener, was aware that the British Expeditionary Force of about 100,000 regulars and reservists was no match for the huge German forces that were pouring westwards. Germany had been able to mobilise 3.8 million men within a week. He had little faith in the territorials with their reputation of being 'part-time soldiers,' and he initially wanted a new volunteer army of 100,000 men. His famous recruiting poster of August 28th 1914 has become one of the iconic symbols of the First World War, supplementing the early efforts of small groups of soldiers who had marched through villages chanting their recruiting ditty: -

"You ought to join Kitcheners's army,
Seven bob a week, plenty of grub to eat,
Great big boots make blisters on your feet,
You ought to join."

(Quoted in *All Quiet on the Home Front* by Richard van Emden and Steven Humphries)

The most iconic recruiting image of World War I.

In spite of the threat of blisters, hundreds of thousands of men besieged recruiting stations across the country. This was reflected locally at an enthusiastic meeting in Hebden Bridge. Posters were put up in every mill and workshop. On September 1st 1914 Todmorden Town Hall hosted a recruiting meeting and within two days 138 men had joined up. R. Thomas and Sons, cotton manufacturers of Hangingroyd, Hebden Bridge, offered £10 to every one of their single male employees who answered the call. The owners of Crossley Mill, Hebden Bridge offered a similar pledge, this time for £5 but linked to a guarantee that the job of every man who enlisted would be there for him when he returned.

It is difficult to ascribe this early enthusiasm solely to motives of duty or honour, along with a desire for 'fair play' to little Belgium. Another explanation for the early rush to recruitment was simply a desire for excitement and adventure, linked to a belief that the war well might be brief and the 'fun' might be missed if action were delayed. At a more practical level, half a million men were made redundant nationally in the first weeks of the war as employers faced economic uncertainty. This must have given the push to many working class men whose poor domestic living conditions may already have made the regular pay and meals of the army seem like an attractive alternative.

There was yet another factor. Anti-German propaganda at the outbreak of war had focused on Prussian militarism and the suspicion that Germany intended to dominate Europe, destroying Britain's trade and Empire in the process. This in itself, along with German spy stories, had provided a wave of anti-German feeling in Britain. This only intensified and aided recruitment. Anti-German feeling was further fuelled by news of the 'Belgian atrocities.' As the Germans had advanced into Belgium they had met some resistance. As a result they had tended to regard all Belgian civilians as real or potential guerrilla fighters and the response was wholly disproportionate to the threat. Towns were burned, civilians used as human shields and hostages shot as reprisals. The events which caused most outrage were the burning of the historic university and library at Louvain and the massacre of over 400 civilians at Tamines. In the first month of the war, over 5,500 civilians were deliberately killed in Belgium and almost 1,000 in France.

These were the facts. Although the pacifist mood of inter-war Britain tended to have them glossed over, and even though the views of

> *Councillor A. Sutcliffe denounced, "the tyranny and barbarism of the German army."*

modern historians tend to vary between seeing these events as a systematic campaign of massacre or simply the excesses of some undisciplined German conscripts, the 'Belgian atrocities' were a gift to British propaganda in the government's recruiting campaign. At a huge recruiting meeting held in September, in Hebden Bridge, Councillor A. Sutcliffe denounced, "the tyranny and barbarism of the German army." Alderman E.J. Crossley followed up by listing some of the German atrocities – firing on the Red Cross, shelling hospitals, violating women, etc. "They are not civilised human beings," he thundered, and added that the Germans would do the same here if ever they invaded. The appeal was for local manhood to protect not only its homeland but its womenfolk too. Warming to this theme, Alderman Crossley appealed to the girls of Hebden Bridge and district, "not to be seen with anyone who has no valid excuses for not going to serve his country." The final touch was added by the Reverend E. Owen who stated that though he hated war, he believed that this was, "a righteous war," in the defence of the Christian principles of right against might and freedom from the brutality of military despotism.

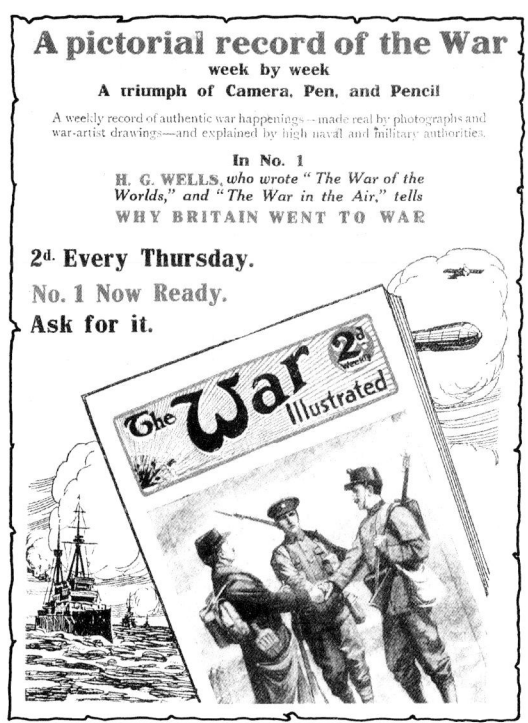

A weekly record of the war – a mixture of fact and propaganda.

Eye-witness accounts from soldiers tended to confirm the ruthless attitude of the Germans towards the Belgian civilians, but their overall impressions of the German foe were not as clear cut. Private Walton Hodgson of Charlestown was recovering from wounds at the house of a relative, Mrs Shepherd of Fern Bank, when he was interviewed by a reporter from the *Todmorden Advertiser*. He spoke of an incident during the retreat from Mons when a little Belgian boy of ten or eleven, fleeing in terror along a street, was shot down and killed by five Germans concealed in a house. Hodgson was clearly enraged at the memory of this incident and spoke of how he and his companions sought and secured revenge. Hodgson also gave a graphic description of his field hospital being shelled, with only the walking wounded able to escape. Those too helpless to escape were left to die, "at the hands of a brutal and merciless enemy."

On the other hand, in terms of 'soldier to soldier' there was sometimes a different story.

Chapter 4 – Appeals and Atrocities

Private Sutcliffe, in the same edition of the *Todmorden Advertiser* that had carried Walton Hodgson's story, recounted his experiences at the Battle of the Aisne and said that he, "saw

> *Lance Corporal Arthur Holmes, of Hebden Bridge was killed on October 20th 1914, but a letter found in his pocket condemned German actions which he had witnessed in Belgium and suggested that the perpetrators should be tied to the front of the British big guns.*

nothing done by the Germans which could be objected to in warfare." Whereas rumours were spreading that the Germans were murdering the British wounded, two soldiers of the local Duke of Wellington's Regiment, who had been taken prisoner and employed to bring in the wounded, later escaped and reported that the behaviour of the Germans had been exemplary. Whilst the *Hebden Bridge Times* reported in full the blood-curdling anti-German speeches

---
Stories were also circulating about German wounded soldiers having their eyes gouged out by Belgian nurses

---

that were made at the huge recruiting meeting of September 1914, it also gave column space to reports of German troops helping British wounded in the field.

Propaganda was of course, not the monopoly of the British. The German press expressed its outrage at the behaviour of those Belgian civilians who were engaging in guerrilla activity. Stories were also circulating about German wounded soldiers having their eyes gouged out by Belgian nurses and Belgian girls slitting the throats of Germans as they slept in their billets. In this welter of accusation and counter accusation there was perhaps one factor which swung the balance of British public opinion heavily against Germany – that was the eye-witness evidence of the 180,000 Belgian refugees who fled to Britain.

The Hebden Bridge Times of November 6th 1914 reported, "wild scenes of enthusiasm," when eight Belgian refugees arrived at Mytholmroyd station to take up residence in the Old Manse attached to the Wesleyan Church. The Manse had been furnished by the people of Mytholmroyd. Some days later Dean House at Luddenden was provided by Mrs Murgatroyd of Broad Fold to provide accommodation for two families from the Antwerp area. This was the beginning of a steady influx of Belgian refugees into the district. Monsieur and Madame Kamps and their two children were found a home in Heptonstall in January 1915. Nineteen more were accommodated in Hebden Bridge – at Heath House, Pleasant View and Market Street. Some of them brought with them dark stories. Madame Kamps had witnessed 15 civilians being lined up and shot. Stories of the plundering of homes by German soldiers were commonplace. A more measured and deliberate act of cruelty was the tale of Belgian civilians being tethered close to big siege guns which were fired by electrical contact from a distance. The concussion waves perforated the ear drums of those forced to stand close by. This was all grist to the mill of the great recruiting campaign that was now in full swing in the Upper Calder Valley.

CHAPTER 5 – SHOULD I STAY OR SHOULD I GO?

Recruiting stations had been besieged after Lord Kitchener's original appeal for 100,000 volunteers. Not all these men would have been accepted as fit for soldiering and the enlistment campaign escalated. By late September 1914 the demand had risen to 500,000 men, and it was in conjunction with this drive that the big recruiting meeting in Hebden Bridge was held in late September. The report of this meeting in the *Hebden Bridge Times* of September 25th 1914 was accompanied by a poster style appeal for about 120 recruits from the '33rd Recruiting Area' to complete the 10th Service Battalion of the West Riding Regiment (an alternative name for the Duke of Wellington's Regiment) and 1,100 'Pals' for the 11th Service Battalion of the same regiment. Recruits were to register at the recruiting office at George Street, Halifax.

Heroes for cigarette smokers to emulate.

The Barracks at Halifax, in Highroad Well, was the headquarters of the man in charge of the '33rd Recruiting Area,' Colonel Thorold. This man was the epitome of an old soldier, and alongside the rousing speeches of Sutcliffe and Crossley, mentioned earlier, Colonel Thorold expressed the hope that a company (around 100 men) could be formed from Hebden Bridge. He stressed the virtues of Yorkshire grit and pluck, qualities that he seemed to have found sadly lacking in the younger generation of Halifax, for he complained of, "young fellows with those beastly cigarettes in their mouths – instead of a good British pipe – skitting at those brave fellows going out."

The immediate results of this recruiting meeting are uncertain, although things were made easier for potential local volunteers by the setting up of a recruiting office in New Road, Hebden Bridge. A rather lame attempt to encourage potential volunteers was the reassurance in the local press that the modern nickel covered bullet, "causes a clean wound, giving an excellent chance of recovery." This sounds rather like giving mice a lecture on the virtues of the speed and efficiency of the mousetrap. Nevertheless on a national scale enlistment had reached 478,893 by late September. One local group who rallied to the flag comprised some old boys of Mytholmroyd Church Lads' Brigade. These were:-

H. Greaves	W. Farrar
W. Taylor	E. Fletcher
C. Longbottom	J.E. Greenwood
L. Waterhouse	H. Thomas
George Harold Clegg	J. Brown
J.E. Wilkinson	Albert Jackson
Arthur Carter	George Hey
Joe Jackson	

Old boys of Mytholmroyd Church Lads' Brigade; off to war in October 1914. Walter Farrar, the uncle of Ted Hughes, is second from left, back row.

A farewell service for the lads was held at St. Michael's Church and they departed to join the King's Own Rifles carrying a gift of 500 cigarettes donated by Mr Geoffrey Robertshaw. Of the thirteen who left on October 4th 1914, four were killed and one died of disease.

Local efforts were stepped up, and in mid-December a recruiting motor tour was organised by the Halifax Civilian Recruiting Committee. A motorcade of over 80 vehicles toured many towns in the West Riding, including those in the Calder Valley. Colonel Thorold was closely involved as was Cragg Vale mill owner, W.A. Simpson-Hinchliffe of Cragg Hall. As an employer of around 300 workpeople, he added another dimension to the German threat by arguing that if the Germans successfully invaded, they would try to destroy the British economy (and jobs) by demolishing mills. A special Footballers' Roll of Honour was established in the *Hebden Bridge Times*, upon which was inscribed the names of volunteers who belonged to local football teams. Among the teams mentioned were Heptonstall Red Star, Hebden United, Hawksclough, and Ridge.

> **Third Line,
> 4th BATTALION DUKE
> OF WELLINGTON'S.**
>
> MEN OF GOOD PHYSIQUE OVER 5ft 1in.
> ARE ACCEPTED FOR THE ABOVE
> BATTALION.
>
> **Enrol at once!**
>
> LOUIS P. FOSTER, MAJOR V.D.,
> OFFICER COMMANDING.
> DRILL HALL, HALIFAX.

A sign of urgent need; the height restriction reduced from 5 foot 6 inches.

Recruiting went on strongly throughout 1915. The height restriction dropped to five feet and one inch in 16 regiments including the

CHAPTER 5 – SHOULD I STAY OR SHOULD I GO

Dukes. Advertisements sometimes targeted specific groups which reflected national military needs. *The Hebden Bridge and District News* for February 26th 1915 carried an appeal for men to become Mechanical Transport Drivers. By the end of the year the same newspaper was printing the army's requests for men to join the Royal Garrison Artillery, an indication of the growing importance of heavy guns in the battles that were raging in France. The scale of local recruiting campaigns became even bigger. On May 22nd 1915 the band of the Duke of Wellington's Regiment (Halifax Territorials) played to large crowds on Market Street, Hebden Bridge, and outside the *White Horse*. The music was supplemented by rousing speeches which urged single young men to join up. All previous campaigns were surpassed by the visit of the 'Flying Column' to the valley on the weekend of September 25th and 26th 1915. No fewer than 500 men of the Duke of Wellington's Territorials marched in full military uniform from Oxenhope to Hebden Bridge on the Saturday, having spent a week recruiting in the Skipton and Craven district, the aim being to enlist 350 men to bring the Sixth Battalion up to strength. They pitched camp on Calder Holmes, stayed overnight and then marched on to Halifax. The visit caused enormous interest throughout the Calder Valley.

How did the single young men of the valley respond to the strenuous attempts to get them into khaki from August 1914 to the end of 1915? There is no doubt that the pressure on them was intense. From the start they were assailed with details of the 'Belgian atrocities' and the prospect of a repeat of such barbarism if ever the Germans reached their homeland. Their manhood was called into question in terms of their unwillingness to defend their womenfolk. At a meeting in Hebden Bridge in April 1915, serving soldiers asked unmarried men in the audience to look to their consciences. How would they feel after the war

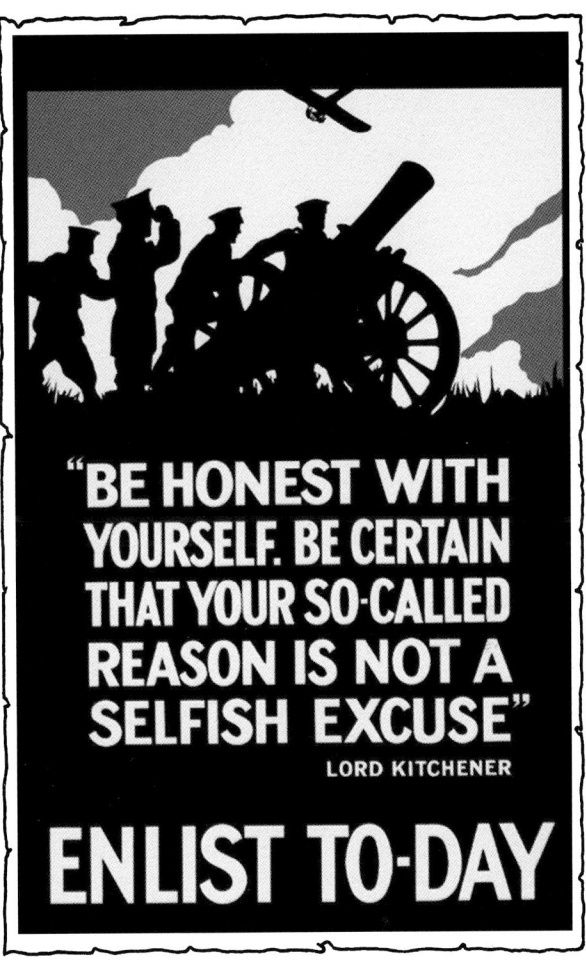

A stream of posters all formed part of an intensive government recruiting campaign.

when people asked them what they had done? At the meeting of May 22nd 1915, outside the *White Horse* in Hebden Bridge, Bandmaster Green of the Dukes went further than this. He bellowed at the large crowd that if young men did not come forward, "they would be fetched," and if conscripted would have to wear a big letter 'C' on their uniforms and be despised by the volunteers.

This campaign of shame was supported by some prominent women at a national level. Baroness Orczy, creator of *The Scarlet Pimpernel*, set up the Women of England's Active Service League, which soon had a membership of 20,000. They pledged to publicly snub any man whom they considered should be in uniform. More radical still was the Order of the White Feather, set up by Charles Fitzgerald but widely supported by women across the country, including such prominent figures as Emmeline and Christabel Pankhurst. Their strident approach was to present a white feather, a symbol of cowardice, to any male considered to be a 'slacker,' accompanied by a verbal harangue. Their approach was sometimes indiscriminate, as boys as young as 15 or 16 could become victims, as well as 40 plus married men, neither group being eligible for enlistment.

were not so clear cut in 1914 and 1915. It was felt wrong, by many of both sexes, that some men went and faced death whilst others stayed at home and allowed the volunteers to make

---

Each card carried a message such as, 'On Service. This house has sent a soldier.'

---

sacrifices. There was another complexity. Married men seemed to be accepting the responsibility of enlisting much more so than single men. During the 'Flying Column' weekend in September 1915, Alderman Crossley speaking on Calder Holmes, described it as a disgrace that around two-thirds of the volunteers so far had been married men. In these circumstances it is perhaps understandable that anger should have been vented in the way that it was, although some of it was misplaced. The local press makes no mention of white feathers being presented, but an item in the *Hebden Bridge and District News* for April 30th 1915 suggests that even houses were being targeted. The report states that the War Office was sending out cards to families with men who were fighting. Each card carried a message such as, 'On Service. This house has sent a soldier,' and could be placed in a window.

Some idea of the Hebden Bridge response to the country's call can be gleaned from an interesting exchange of letters in the *Hebden Bridge Times*. In February 1915 a Mr Sainsbury of Clitheroe, formerly a resident of Hebden Bridge, wrote to the newspaper suggesting that the men of the town had responded poorly to the recruiting drive. Rather surprisingly, the riposte came from a soldier, Sam Jackson, a member of the Dukes in training at Doncaster. Sam's letter of March 5th 1915 defends the lads of Hebden Bridge by stating that most of them were working hard in factories making clothing for servicemen and in this way 'doing their bit' for the country. Sam then adopted a different

Women were called upon to increase the pressure.

With hindsight, and with full knowledge of the appalling slaughter of the trenches, it now seems incredible that women should have been pressurising men in this way. The moral issues

angle, suggesting that some were desperate to join up and fight, but had a domestic duty that spoke more strongly than patriotism. He couched this in a poem, four lines of which ran as follows,

"His country called, his heart responded 'Yes.'

But duty's voice rang louder, yet more shrill:

'You are your mother's sole support and stay,

You cannot leave her lonely, weak and ill.'"

Sam's letter was met with one which expressed both incredulity and contempt in the next issue of the newspaper. The correspondent, who signs himself only 'F.G.', wonders first of all if Sam's letter is an exercise in sarcasm. Putting this aside, 'F.G.' launches a blistering attack on the district's 'slackers.' He claims that hundreds of young men in the Calder Valley, in their prime and unmarried, are simply not doing their duty. According to 'F.G.', the explanation of government contracts for khaki is just an excuse. Home responsibilities are similarly dismissed. "Pampered at home, lolling at entertainments, watching or playing football, they have no thoughts beyond: what can they know of responsibility?" 'F.G.' signs off with stating that the liberty of the country is at stake. Two months later, in May 1915, a letter from Trooper C.B. Robinson, with the 2nd Life Guards in Belgium, and written to a friend in Heptonstall, very much echoed the sentiments of 'F.G.' He stated that he was ashamed at the low recruitment numbers from Hebden Bridge, and that there wouldn't be so many 'slackers' if the people at home realised that, "liberty and freedom are at stake."

The truth concerning recruitment in the Upper Calder Valley probably lies somewhere between the views of Sam Jackson on the one hand and 'F.G.' and Trooper Robinson on the other hand. If 'F.G.' had access to official figures he made no mention of them. He seems to have based his conclusions on his Saturday night observations on the streets of various local towns. He may well have been right about low recruitment figures locally, but he was wrong to believe that large government

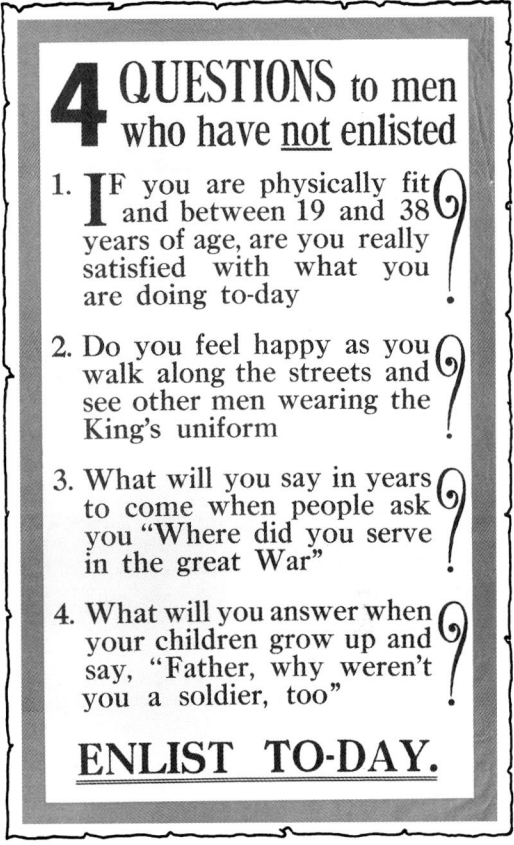

Men were asked to search their consciences.

contracts for army and navy clothing had no connection with recruitment. Mr J. H. Levi was the man in charge at the Hebden Bridge Recruiting Office, at Hope Street. Over the course of the 49 weeks from December 1914, 350 Hebden Royd men signed up here. His returns during 1915 show a handful of volunteers coming forward weekly – usually five or six; one week as low as one. However, during the week preceding May 7th an amazing spike took place. No fewer than 55 men enlisted. Mr Levi accorded great credit for this phenomenon to the firm of J.B. Hoyle and Co., praising its generosity to its employees who had enlisted and singling out the head of the firm for his great encouragement to those who were eligible. More than this, only two of the 55 had left a wife and children behind. This group was to suffer a relatively high death rate as 21 failed to survive.

A parade passes Crossley Mill, whose owners offered £5 to any of its unmarried men who enlisted early in the war.
Courtesy of the Jack Uttley Photo Library

It is probable that some of the generosity of J.B. Hoyle and Co. included financial incentives to men to enlist. Other local firms had been doing this since September 1914. The firm of R. Thomas and Sons of Hangingroyd, Hebden Bridge, for example, had offered the sum of £10 to any single man from its workforce. This was a substantial amount considering the wages of that time in local textiles. J.B. Hoyle and Co. were perhaps doing that bit more, for Mr Levi gives the impression that many of the 55 new recruits came from that factory, and perhaps there was a sense of 'all in it together lads,' something akin to the spirit of the 'Pals' battalions raised in small industrial towns. However, another press comment of that time spoke of local firms getting on top of army and navy clothing contracts. This suggests another reason for the recruitment spike. Times had been relatively prosperous for local workers, but future government orders could never be guaranteed. It is probable that this batch of young men decided to take the plunge because the prospect now was of firms shedding jobs. At any rate the recruits left in two parties, the first one of 20 to 25 departing from Hebden

'Are We Downhearted? No!'

Bridge station and cheered off by a large crowd. The boys themselves were in good spirits, singing 'Are We Downhearted? No!'

The dilemma of 'Should I stay or should I go?' was not destined to last much longer. The idea of conscription was controversial but had been in the air from the very outset of war. A letter in the *Hebden Bridge Times* for September 4th 1914 struck a rare jarring note with regard to the war effort, but was remarkably prescient. The correspondent, signing off as 'Y.Z.', states that it is the poor homes which are most liberal with their sons. "Some have to starve or enlist." He accuses local employers of bribing their workers to enlist, whereas they should be setting an example by sending their sons first. What some may have seen as class war, 'Y.Z.' describes as fair play. He sees the answer in conscription to ensure that, "every class will be doing its share." The idea gathered momentum, albeit for different reasons. One Captain Walkley, speaking at a recruiting meeting in Manchester in February 1915, warned that conscription was inevitable unless more single men did not come forward quickly. It was simply a matter of numbers. The army needed more and more men. The great recruiting meetings in the Calder Valley hammered home the same message – come or be fetched. *The Hebden Bridge Times* of June 4th 1915 carried an editorial which reverted to the issue of fairness from two points of view – firstly, that married men were carrying an undue burden of responsibility in terms of volunteering; secondly, that territorials were being called on to serve abroad despite the fact that they had been brought into being for Home Defence. National Service was the only answer. One way or another, for one reason or another, conscription was on its way.

CHAPTER 6 – SHOULDERS TO THE WHEEL

At the outbreak of war, Councillor A. Sutcliffe had made dire predictions that the disruptions to world trade would mean distress and unemployment for Hebden Bridge. Perhaps to his surprise the opposite was true, initially at

Redmans at Foster Mill enjoyed huge contracts for the making of duffel coats for the navy.
Courtesy of the Jack Uttley Photo Library

least. After all, this was 'Fustianopolis,' nationally known as a home to ready-made clothing, an industry, which could easily be converted to the needs of the nation at war. In September 1914 lucrative government army contracts came into the town. The local press calculated that the demand was for two million khaki uniforms, one million heavy serge coats, 250,000 cotton bed ticks and pillowcases and half a million haversacks for the French army. Foster Mill (Redmans), Hebden Bridge, received a separate contract for duffel coats for the navy. The large firms who received the contracts distributed the work amongst other local firms and so the weaving sheds, the cutting rooms, the sewing shops and dye-works of the district were soon hives of activity. Large blanket mills at Mytholmroyd also benefited from these contracts which, it is estimated, would keep local factories busy for at least six months.

If then, Colonel Thorold and other driving forces behind the great recruiting campaigns felt that their efforts fell on somewhat stony ground in this area, here was at least one explanation. The textiles industry in the Upper Calder Valley had suffered its share of trade depressions since the later nineteenth century with the resultant unemployment or short-time working. These army contracts presented a golden opportunity for work and plenty of it, including overtime. Doubtless many single young men in the weaving sheds, dye-houses and cutting rooms, were not prepared to swap this for army pay of seven shillings per week, and a very uncertain future when a weaver, for example, could earn much more. For married men the separation allowance for wives was raised from just over eleven shillings per week to twelve and sixpence, with an extra allowance of two shillings per child, but this was not really adequate. If the recruiters pressed home the argument of duty and honour, as opposed to purely economic considerations, these local textile workers could argue that they were indeed 'putting their shoulders to the wheel' in terms of the war effort because uniforms were essential.

Immaculate from top to toe. Arthur Barker of Mytholmroyd stands second from the right.
Courtesy of Peter Robertshaw

The importance of uniforms was backed by the highest authority. In December 1914 a card notice was placed prominently in all local clothing concerns showing an extract from a letter written by the Secretary of War, Lord Kitchener, to the Wholesale Manufacturing Confederation. The extract urged clothing workers to the utmost effort in manufacturing army clothing and, tellingly, stated the following,

"In carrying out the great work of providing the Army with its equipment, employers and employees alike are doing their duty for their king and country, equally with those who have joined the Army for service in the field." The problem was that the government service contracts tended to fluctuate as much as the trade cycle. When one was finished there was

> "Ordinary business is now at low ebb. Full employment may be difficult."

no guarantee of when (if ever) another would arrive, which explains fluctuations in local recruiting prior to conscription. For example, the editorial in the *Hebden Bridge Times* for September 10th 1914 is a mixture of anxiety and optimism as it speaks of rumoured large new orders for military clothing to be placed in the West Riding. The hope expressed is that Hebden Bridge will get its share because although small army orders came regularly, big orders were now needed. Khaki contracts had almost run out and French and Russian orders were nearing completion. "Ordinary business is now at low ebb. Full employment may be difficult."

In national terms the war economy was so dependent on industry that the workers were put in a powerful bargaining position. However, the need for some harmony in industrial relations caused the trades union leaders to accept the Treasury Agreement (1915) with the government. The principle of 'dilution' was established by which unskilled and female labour could take over jobs which had traditionally been done by men, many of whom were now entering the armed forces. As a result, in the course of the war just over 1.5 million women took over men's jobs. This social phenomenon had less impact in the Calder Valley than in many other areas for female working in textiles had long been the 'norm.' The clothing trade in Hebden Bridge, for example, gave employment to about 2,500 people, mainly women and girls as machinists. Sewing shops were busy putting together the garments from the cloth provided by the weavers, and even half of these were women. Machinists and finishers were on piece rates and the very highly skilled females could earn 26 to 30 shillings per week. Female labour was crucial to family incomes in the valley, particularly as many married women went out to work. This put women in a strong social and economic position locally, the reverse of the coin being that during trade depressions two or more adults in a family could face unemployment.

Christmas 1915 in the sewing shop of Hartley's Linden Works, Hebden Bridge.
Courtesy of Pennine Horizons

Chapter 6 – Shoulders To The Wheel

Women railway carriage cleaners at Sowerby Bridge. *Courtesy of Stephen Gee*

Textiles may have been the staple local industry, but it was not the only one. A sprinkling of engineering firms could be found along the valley and they enjoyed government contracts for the making of machinery and small parts. This was a field in which women certainly were newcomers and were 'putting their shoulders to the wheel' both here and on the railways. On July 2nd 1915, the *Hebden Bridge Times* announced that shell making was to commence in the town shortly. In August an advertisement in the local press requested lodgings for munitions volunteers coming to work at Ormerod Bros. of Valley Road, Hebden Bridge. The request was classed as 'urgent' and suggests that people were coming into the town from further afield. The importance of munitions was such that in October 1915 the General Munitions Tribunal at Halifax fined the firm of Thomas H. Pickles (Iron founders) of Mytholmroyd five pounds with one guinea costs for 'poaching' a workman, William Dransfield of Midgley, from Haxby and Co., Halifax, a firm wholly engaged in munitions work.

By September 1915 Ormerods of Hebden Bridge was engaged in the production of shells, and women were part of the workforce. Effective artillery was now deemed as essential if the stalemate on the Western Front was to be broken. A shell shortage scandal had erupted in 1915 and Lloyd George at the Ministry of Munitions was determined to drive forward shell production. It was part of this drive which brought the local M.P., Mr Holmes, to Ormerods in November 1915. He was accompanied by Mr Simpson-Hinchliffe J.P., of Cragg Hall in Cragg Vale, a man untiring in his efforts to promote the war effort. Both men spoke of the urgent need for more shells and appealed to the workers for greater efforts in order to aid France, Russia and, "our gallant lads at the Front." The shell shortage was overcome and levels of production remained high in what was virtually a new industry. With fewer and fewer men available, munitions work became dominated by women, and this was no doubt true at Ormerods. Women could earn good money in munitions, but there were risks to health and other dangers. In the most disastrous episode, 134 workers were killed at a munitions factory explosion at Chilwell, Nottingham, in July 1918. Nothing on that scale happened locally, although in December 1917 an explosion in a munitions factory at nearby Copley killed one and injured two more.

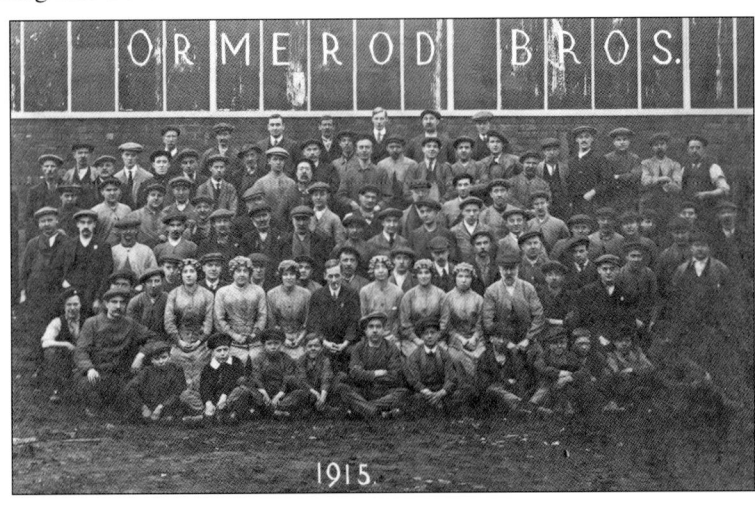

The need for shells was desperate in 1915. *Courtesy of Pennine Horizons*

If times were relatively good for local industry during 1914 and 1915, there were suspicions in some quarters that times were a little too good for some. At the outbreak of war, the government had issued an assurance that there would be no need for prices to rise. By the end of 1915 the cost of living was increasing at a rate of 27% per annum. Wages in most sectors could not keep up. There were other concerns too. Whilst there was much sympathy for the Belgian refugees coming into the district, a local meeting of the Labour Party in December 1914 discussed a circular published by the Sowerby Division of the Party. This stressed its opposition to any use of the Belgians as cheap labour. Not only this, it opposed the use of Belgian labour in any local trade where there was unemployment or part-time working, also insisting that if trade dropped, "none of our own people must be turned away so long as refugees are employed." Some themes are ever contemporary.

It was prices, however, that caused most concern, not the possible economic

The prices of milk and bread were the chief targets of complaint

competition of the Belgian refugees. Mention has already been made of the turbulent meeting of the Todmorden and District Trades and Labour Council, held at the Weavers' Institute in February 1915. The prices of milk and bread were the chief targets of complaint, along with a more generalised outrage at the profiteering of monopolists. The language used was violent but the answer, at least in the eyes of the meeting, was simple – government control of both food supply and prices. A big May Day Demonstration organised by the Trades Council and Labour organisations of Sowerby Bridge brought forth speeches regretting that whilst the working classes were making great sacrifices on behalf of the nation, unity and victory could only be achieved if the government moved to protect working class living standards.

The press, though solidly patriotic in general, expressed much unease over this issue. The editorial of the *Yorkshire Observer* for April 30th 1915 had 'WAR PROFITS' as its headline. It argued that it was not in arms manufacture that excess profits were being made but elsewhere. It gave as an example a large flour milling firm in South Wales where

the lawns of Ascot and Epsom were thronged with merry, irresponsible and careless pleasure seekers

profits had increased fourfold from the previous year and dividends were up by 20%. "It is intolerable that such large profits can be drawn from the necessities of the poor." Similarly the *Hebden Bridge Times*, not known for summoning people to the barricades, lamented in April 1915 that the Ascot and Epsom race meetings were proceeding as usual. "Our only hope is that it will not be the lot of history to record that, while the British legions were struggling across the Channel against an implacable foe, the lawns of Ascot and Epsom were thronged with merry, irresponsible and careless pleasure seekers who seemed oblivious of the fact that their countryman were fighting and dying to keep their homes inviolate."

Strong words indeed, and although this same newspaper dutifully reported the 'Glorious Twelfth' and the start of the grouse shooting season in August, the implication was almost that the local gentry might be making better use of their guns elsewhere. At least, the newspaper reported, "most of the birds are likely to find their way into military hospitals." Also it seemed to some that that if any curbs were to be placed on pleasures, then the target would be working class pleasures. In August 1914 Lloyd George had stated that drink was a deadlier foe than any German or Austrian. A war tax on beer was imposed and the opening hours of public houses were regulated. Lloyd George was probably not opposed to strong drink for its own sake, but did not want men or women lingering in pubs when they could be out working for the war effort. Therefore the carefree days of pubs remaining open from 5.30 a.m. to 12.30 a.m. the following day were over, as by 1915 the opening hours were restricted to midday to 2.30 p.m. and 6.30 p.m. to 9.30 p.m. Not only this, alcohol was diluted by law.

> *On April 16th 1915 the Hebden Bridge Times printed a rather doleful picture of how the new laws affected the locality on the first day of their coming into operation. At one public house, at 9.30 p.m. precisely, the entire company rose as one man, sang 'The Doxology,' and then departed. The newspaper gives no hint as to how much irony, if any, was inserted into this Christian prayer.*

In theory pubs could stay open after 9.30 p.m. for the sale of non-intoxicating drink, but a half-hearted experiment in this direction was soon abandoned locally. These government measures had originally been aimed, for obvious reasons, at centres of munitions production. Now they applied nationally and although unpopular they worked. Discipline at work was better and domestic violence declined. Arrests for drunkenness decreased, and not just in the male population. The figures for women nationally declined from around 40,000 in 1914 to around 25,000 in 1917. This was all to the good, but as the war really began to bite on the Home Front in 1915, the outlook for working class men became even gloomier with the stoppage of professional football and cricket by the end of that year.

CHAPTER 7 – THEY ALSO SERVE

For those not in the fighting services, or engaged in war contract work in factories, there were other ways in which to serve the country through volunteer or charity work. From the outset of the conflict, War Distress Funds were set up in all the local townships. The Hebden Bridge War Distress Fund kicked off on August 21st 1914 with initial contributions totalling £590. One week later the fund stood at just over £898. By December 4th 1914, having taken Heptonstall into its ambit, the fund stood at £2326. Mytholmroyd, Luddenden Foot and Midgley had their own funds. The supporters of these funds were a mixture of local worthies, councillors and manufacturers. Parts of church and chapel collections began to be directed towards these funds. Employee collections played a part. These were usually voluntary and irregular, but things were put on a more regular basis at Acre Mill, the home of James Hoyle and Sons. From August 29th 1914 the workpeople there agreed to a levy of 3d (roughly 1p) in the £ on their weekly wages in support of the Hebden Bridge Fund.

The initial aim of the War Distress Funds was to support war widows, the families of serving soldiers and the men themselves should they be invalided out. However, almost immediately another needy group was identified when Belgian refugees arrived in the district, some of them possessing little more than the clothes they stood up in. The first batch of eight arrived at Mytholmroyd station in early November 1914, being housed at the Old Manse attached to the Wesleyan Church. Their plight aroused great sympathy on the part of local people and the Manse was entirely furnished by the residents of Mytholmroyd. Another two families arrived a few days later and were set up at Dean House in Luddenden. In January 1915 nineteen refugees were accommodated in Hebden Bridge at Heath House, Pleasant View and Market Street.

As a result, unusual names began to crop up amongst the regulation Greenwoods and Sutcliffes of the locality. For example, Monsieur Saylor Peterus, head of a family of six, was installed by the friends of Salem at Heath Bank, Hebden Bridge. At the same time the friends of Hope Baptist Church and School, having promised to maintain a party of Belgian refugees, welcomed Madame Van Gerven and her son and daughter to their new home at Cliffe House. They were accompanied by Monsieur Leon Bernard and his wife, whilst Monsieur Carpentier completed the group. The log book of Hebden Bridge National School (now Hebden Royd Primary School) shows some interesting new names appearing on the register. On 11th June 1917, Joseph T. Mortier, son of Philemon Mortier of 30 King Street, a munitions worker, and Carolina Peynshaert, daughter of Sivesin Peynshaert of 14 King Street, Hebden Bridge, appear in the school log book. Gerard Joseph Vermeir and Vicktoria Francisca Vermeir appear on 16th October 1917 listed as the children of Karel Camille Vermeir and living at 26 Green Syke.

Help at home for those made needy by the war.

The school log book of Hebden Bridge National School had never seen names such as 'Vermeir' before.

Many of the newcomers to Hebden Bridge not only spoke of the destruction they had witnessed but also the savagery of the invading German forces, thus reinforcing the stories of the 'Belgian atrocities' so widely published in the British press. As a result local Distress Funds now included sections specifically dedicated to Belgian Relief and Distress in Belgium. By May 1915 the former fund at Hebden Bridge had raised £933 and the following surnames appeared on the donors list: - Kamps, Geerunkx, Mortier, Verreyken, Rosseel, Zeileman and Peynshaert. Clearly the early arrivals were doing their bit to help the unfortunates who were still arriving.

If helping the Belgian refugees was not directly aiding the war effort, it was at least strengthening the idea that the Germans were a pitiless and ruthless foe and that every effort had to be made to defeat them. This reinforced the government's message that self-sacrifice of

> *an appeal was made to the women of England to sign a pledge committing them to limit their purchases of luxuries*

the fighting men should be matched by the self-sacrifice of civilians in every way possible. For one group of aristocratic ladies this meant the establishment of the Women's War Economy League. In a circular to the press carrying the signatures of such illustrious figures as the Marchioness of Ripon, the Countess of Pembroke and Lady Juliet Duff, an appeal was made to the women of England to sign a pledge committing them to limit their purchases of luxuries, especially imports; to resist new fashions in dress; to give up all unnecessary entertainments, both at home and in restaurants and to avoid, "as far as possible the use of motors."

The appeal was well-meaning but couched in language that allowed of interpretation according to economic circumstances and lifestyle. What was, for example, a necessary entertainment? At a more humble level the womenfolk of the Calder Valley felt no undue strain at resisting luxuries, restaurants and the use of motor cars. Instead they pitched in at a more practical level. Whilst the female workforce was hard at it on government contracts in sewing shops, women with more leisure time on their hands were joining voluntary organisations in aid of the war effort. In January 1915 the Hebden Bridge branch of the British Red Cross reported that it had dispatched the following to the Field Force Fund – 92 pairs of socks, 52 scarfs, 30 pairs of mittens and cuffs, 19 balaclava helmets and 4 caps. To the headquarters of the Red Cross were sent 24 towels, 12 jerseys, 11 shirts, 8 body belts, 7 pairs of slippers, 2 pairs of bed socks and 1 pair of operation stockings. Whilst these items had been collected locally, the local

Red Cross members had also busied themselves making 120 roller bandages and 156 slings. These too were dispatched to headquarters. The following month the organisation made an appeal for small, rough towels, to be sent to the front as the fighting men got so filthy and wet in the trenches.

> *A sign that the war in Europe was taking an ominous turn for the worse was revealed in the new work that the Hebden Bridge Red Cross was engaged in from April 1915 – making simple respirators for protection against gas. These consisted of an oblong patch of bleached absorbent cotton wool and three layers of bleached cotton gauze to go over the mouth and nostrils. Held in place by a band around the head, these primitive devices had to serve until the later introduction of proper gas masks.*

There were other ways of helping the Red Cross and, indirectly, the lads at the front. A popular method of raising funds was through the medium of concerts. Two were given at Christmas 1914 in the Co-operative Hall, Hebden Bridge, by the Choral and Harmonic Society combined with the Male Voice Choir. Whilst one of the concerts presented the traditional Christmas offering of the 'Messiah,' the other doubled up as both fund raiser and recruiting call. Mr Walter Sayer, for example, sang *The Young Soldier Boy*, whilst *Fall In*, presented by the popular local vocalist, Herbert Greenwood, was, "a stirring, candid recruiting call." The evening concluded with enthusiastic renditions of *Rule Britannia* and *Land of Hope and Glory* by both audience and performers.

People rallied to the cause in their own way, some of them a little unusual. The staff of Holts, a shop which still stands proudly at the corner of Bridge Gate and New Road in Hebden Bridge, collected 175 walking sticks for wounded soldiers. The *Hebden Bridge Times* of August 6th 1915 was full of praise for two little boys from High Street, Arthur Nutter and Wilfred Gibson, who had collected three shillings and eight pence by selling lavender bags and badges in aid of the Wounded Soldiers' Fund. A later scheme for helping wounded soldiers by collecting eggs was set up nationally in 1916, and in the April of that year the children of Crimsworth Council School proudly announced that they had collected 743 eggs over the month.

Support for soldiers wounded in the cause of king and country carried great emotional resonance and civilians were eager to offer whatever they could. Ambition ran high in Todmorden where the decision was made to set up a military hospital at Centre Vale Mansion, formerly belonging to the powerful Fielden

Centre Vale Military Hospital, Todmorden – an imposing retreat for wounded soldiers. J.A. Lee

family but now in the hands of the town council. It was recognised from the start that the flow of military casualties would put great strain on the regular hospital services, and auxiliary hospitals were opened all over the country. Centre Vale Military Hospital was one of these, the first patients arriving in November 1914. Doctor J. Lawson Russell was in charge and many of the nurses were local volunteers. Indeed, although the hospital received government grants, it was largely sustained through public subscriptions and fund raising events. By the time the hospital closed in 1919 it had treated over one thousand servicemen. A more detailed description of its work can be found in Chapter 16 of this book.

Some of the nurses who served in military hospitals at home could volunteer to work in the various theatres of war. Along with ambulance men, these were the people who wore uniforms but carried no weapons, serving near or at the front line, with all its attendant dangers. The war induced a great boost in the recruitment of ambulancemen. The Hebden Bridge Corps of the St. John Ambulance Brigade provided a healthy stream of recruits to serve abroad, many of them being incorporated into the R.A.M.C. (Royal Army Medical Corps), and in January 1915, fourteen left to take up their duties. One of the earlier volunteers served on the hospital ship *Oxfordshire* which carried casualties across the Channel from France. In a cheerful letter home,

---

It is possible that they were blissfully unaware of what awaited them, but they soon found out.

---

he described celebrating Christmas Day 1914 at sea and his arrival at Boulogne where a 'smoking concert' was enjoyed.

If there were dangers from German 'U'-boats at sea, then some ambulancemen found themselves in areas where the fighting was very hot indeed. The *Hebden Bridge Times* for March 1915 reported that three local ambulance men – Privates Sutcliffe, Stansfield and Naylor – all attached to the Royal Army Medical Corps (Naval Division) had sailed for Egypt on board the Canadian ship *Royal George*. A letter from Private Sutcliffe commented on the good food and comfortable beds aboard ship. It is possible that they were blissfully unaware of what awaited them, but they soon found out. Their ultimate destination was Gallipoli, and in a graphic letter home in July 1915, Private Stansfield described just how difficult it was to deal with heavy casualties in trench warfare, particularly in the searing heat of an East-Mediterranean summer. Later in the war at least one local ambulance man was to die whilst on stretcher bearing duties.

Whilst ambulancemen brought the wounded off the battlefield, having first treated them as best they could, it was the task of the nurses to deal with the casualties in field dressing stations or in military hospitals behind the lines. To serve abroad in this way was purely voluntary, but there seems to have been no shortage of nurses ready to go out and face work that they must have known would be harrowing, and in in some cases, dangerous. An early local recruit was Miss Anne Brotherton of Lees Road, Hebden Bridge. She had been connected with Salem Wesleyan Church and at the outbreak of war was a nursing sister at Salisbury Infirmary. By the end of 1914 she had been accepted by the War Office for service at the front and was on her way to France.

Clearly the work took its toll on her, for in a letter home written in June 1915, Miss Brotherton reported that she had been invalided from duty for three weeks, "after two months strenuous work in a fever division." She spent the three weeks in Britain at 'Cornelot,' a residence loaned by the Duchess of Argyle to be used as a rest home for run-down sisters. Sister Brotherton was soon back in the thick of things on her return to France, and she described as heart-breaking the sight of hundreds of gassed and wounded men (mainly Canadians) flooding into camp hospitals after some severe fighting around Ypres. With quite unnecessary apologies for the infrequency of her letters, Sister Brotherton signed off by saying that at the end of her day's work she was just too tired for writing. "My correspondence is dreadfully neglected, but I am sure they [her friends] will understand." I feel sure that they did!

> *By August 1916 Sister Brotherton was working on one of a flotilla of barges that worked the canals to bring the most seriously wounded men from camp hospitals to base hospitals in France. The gentler motion of the barges was thought more suitable for critically wounded men than ambulance trains. In a letter home Sister Brotherton described an incident, a week earlier, when her barge was waiting at a camp hospital for the transfer of its, "crushed and broken humanity," to the barge. At this point the German artillery began to pound the nearby town and one shell fell on the casualty hospital. Nobody was killed, but it was with the greatest difficulty and danger that sixty of the worst cases were transferred to the barge.*

Sister Brotherton was seeing both the best and worst of humanity, but she was trenchant in her condemnation of, "this unholy war and all the suffering and misery it has caused." She

She and her fellow nurses managed to deal with 11,000 wounded men in ten days

ended her letter by saying how saddened she had been at hearing of the loss of so many Hebden Bridge boys. She was to be awarded the Mons Medal in May 1918.

There was no doubt that nurses themselves could have a rough time of it. Nurse S.E. Wadsworth wrote to her sister, Mrs Hargreaves of Crown Street, Hebden Bridge, in February 1915. Stationed at Calais, Miss Wadsworth at first had to sleep on a mattress in a barn with seventeen other nurses, sharing one wash basin and one looking glass. There was not even a chair to sit on and clothes had to be left in suitcases. This lasted ten days until better accommodation could be found. She and her fellow nurses managed to deal with 11,000 wounded men in ten days before dispatching them off to hospital ships. Nurse Wadsworth had heard stories of German atrocities, but she showed the true face of compassion when coming across German casualties. "Some of them looked pretty frightened, so we were as kind as possible to them, because a wounded man is a wounded man after all."

Conditions at Calais had been difficult for both nurses and casualties at first, with the wounded simply lying around everywhere. Even when a college was commandeered and turned into a hospital, there were only three enamel cups for each ward at first. Thankfully the British Red Cross Society soon remedied matters by sending supplies. Nurse Wadsworth turned out to be a dedicated professional and towards the end of the war she was to be awarded the Royal Red Cross for her services in Mesopotamia, having begun active service in France in October 1914.

> **THE HUMAN TOUCH**
> *Nurses had to harden themselves to the spectacle of terrible injuries and to witnessing the deaths of many young men during the war. However, a nurse at a military hospital in Brighton must have been particularly touched by the case of Robert Greenwood of 7 Weavers' Square, Heptonstall. He died from shell wounds to the abdomen in August 1917 and the nurse sent a lock of his hair to his mother.*

One of the most interesting voluntary groups in the field was the Friends Ambulance Unit. The Society of Friends, otherwise known as the Quakers, had completely pacifist ideals but its members could be seen on the Western Front attempting to alleviate the miseries of war inflicted on civilians. Having raised their own funds, young Quakers drained wells and tested water supplies; re-interred the dead if they posed a health threat; repaired cottages and provided boots, clothing and money to homeless and starving villagers.

Meanwhile as 1915 drew to a close, the Upper Calder Valley looked back on the first full year of war. On the positive side of the balance sheet, there must have been some satisfaction at the wholehearted efforts of local volunteers and charity workers to aid the war effort in various ways. The annual audit of the Hebden Bridge and District War Distress Fund revealed not only direct help to needy families of serving soldiers, but also support to organisations which were directly helping servicemen, such as the Red Cross, the Y.M.C.A., the Prisoner of War Fund and the Centre Vale Military Hospital in Todmorden. As if this wasn't enough, the Distress Fund donated money to Belgian refugees, to civilians in Belgium, to Armenian refugees and to Polish victims of the war.

On the negative side of the balance sheet was the increasingly uncomfortable feeling that it was not just foreign civilians who faced

In December 1914 German cruisers bombarded the east coast towns of Hartlepool, Bridlington, Scarborough and Whitby, killing a number of civilians.

danger. In December 1914 German cruisers bombarded the east coast towns of Hartlepool, Bridlington, Scarborough and Whitby, killing a number of civilians. This caused national outrage and anti-German feeling, as did the sinking of the Cunard passenger liner, *Lusitania*, by a German 'U–boat off the coast of Ireland in May 1915, with a loss of 1,198 lives. Even so, the citizens of the Upper Calder Valley could feel relatively safe from any naval threat. A threat from the air, however, was a different matter. As early as October 1914,

mention of the 'Zeppelin Peril' was being made in the local press. These monster sized airships loomed large in the imaginations of the British public, but tended to be dismissed by the authorities as inefficient and with limited range.

A MEDAL FOR A MEDIC

Walter Jackson of Hangingroyd, Hebden Bridge, probably had no visions of heroism whilst doing his duties as a member of the Royal Army Medical Corps on board the hospital ship **Oxfordshire***. However, he found himself in the thick of the action when the ship* **Tycheus** *was torpedoed by a German 'U' boat. The crew of the* **Oxfordshire** *found themselves on a rescue mission as they endeavoured to save the seamen from the stricken* **Tycheus***. In doing so, four of the* **Oxfordshire's** *crew won the Military Medal, one of them being Walter Jackson.*

However, matters had to be taken more seriously with the first Zeppelin raid on Britain, bombs being dropped on Great Yarmouth on January 19th 1915. On June 4th 1915 the first Zeppelin raid on Yorkshire took place – at Driffield – and 25 people were killed in a raid on Hull. It must have come as a still greater shock to the Calder Valley when news came of Zeppelin attacks on East Lancashire towns. The Zeppelin in question was heard overhead locally on the night of September 26th 1916. Its target was Manchester but, missing his way, the pilot dropped bombs on Bury and Bolton. The explosions could be heard in Todmorden. The local press carried official instruction as to how to behave during a Zeppelin raid in February 1915, advice being laid down with regard to a variety of locations – streets, homes, business premises, schools and chapels. In May 1915 public notices in the press were warning local people that gas supplies would be cut off in the event of an air raid.

Chapter 7 – They Also Serve

> **HEBDEN BRIDGE AND MYTHOLMROYD GAS BOARD.**
> Gas Offices, Carlton Street,
> Hebden Bridge, April 20th, 1915.
>
> ## War Risks.--Warning.
>
> NOTICE IS HEREBY GIVEN that the GAS SUPPLY may be CUT OFF at the Gas Works at any moment, and it is necessary that all users of gas should take notice that Gas Taps, and particularly the Meter Taps, should be SHUT OFF immediately warning is given, and not turned on again until similar notice is again given that the supply is ready for use.
>
> WARNING will be given as quickly as possible by the sounding of Fire Buzzers at the following places:—
>
> Fire Buzzer, Gas Works, Crow Nest, Hebden Bridge.
> Fire Buzzer, Messrs. Ratcliffe Bros., Green Hill, Mytholmroyd.
> Fire Buzzer, Messrs. J. Hoyle, Ltd., Acre Mill, Old Town.
> Fire Buzzer, Messrs. Mitchell Bros., Boston Hill, Old Town.
>
> The sounding will be operated intermittently for five minutes.
>
> IT IS ESSENTIAL THAT ALL GAS CONSUMERS EXAMINE THE METER TAPS AT ONCE TO SEE THAT THEY ARE IN ORDER. IF THEY REQUIRE ATTENTION NOTIFICATION SHOULD BE SENT TO THE ABOVE ADDRESS WITHOUT DELAY, AND THEY WILL BE ATTENDED TO.
>
> (Signed)
> R. CRABTREE, Clerk to the Board.
> E. J, WELLENS, Engineer and Manager.

The great fear was zeppelins.

No attack from the air ever fell on the Calder Valley during this war, although the threat of it must have increased the gloom as the winter months set in towards the end of 1915. There was gloom more literally speaking because lighting restrictions had been in force since February as a result of the aerial threat. At first the restrictions were at the discretion of the military authorities and could range from a full blackout to just dimming of the lights. At any event all lighted roof areas had to be covered over or lighting intensity reduced to a minimum. This produced a particular problem for Hebden Bridge with mills working day and night on government contracts. There was plenty of glass in these mills, both on roofs and sides, and the *Hebden Bridge Times* pointed out that this was not only a problem at night but also in the early mornings and evenings when the reflected glare of lighting could be seen at a great distance.

Local manufacturers tended to vary in their responses, but in February 1916 the Lighting Order was imposed and all light had to be blacked out during the hours of darkness. Not only mill owners, but also tradesmen and house owners had to put up dark blinds. Street lighting was reduced to a minimum. Churches and chapels generally replaced their evening services with afternoon ones. Lighting restrictions were just one more pinprick in a life that had become increasingly regimented and controlled since the passing of D.O.R.A. (Defence of the Realm Act) at the very outset of war. This gave the government huge powers, including the right to imprison people without trial, seize land for the war effort and impose press censorship so rigorous that it was forbidden, "to report news that was liable to cause alarm and despondency."

> *D.O.R.A. regulated life down to the smallest detail. It was no longer permitted to give bread to horses, buy binoculars (fear of spies) or fly kites and light bonfires. Either of these last two, it was suspected, could be used to send signals to the enemy. If this was a little far-fetched, then bonfires could legitimately be seen both as a waste of precious fuel and a 'magnet' for Zeppelins.*

In times of adversity or danger the British often resort to humour as a release. The newspapers were well aware of this and began to print quirky stories as an antidote to the growing pressures of the war on the Home Front. A reporter from the *Spectator* was said to have overheard a woman in the East End of London saying that her son was, "driving a motor in the mountainous part of Paris." A Hampshire farm labourer solemnly announced that, "Our Bill is in the Sewage Canal because o' them Turkeys." If the latter was a patronising view of country yokels, it might well have been one that was shared by the relatively sophisticated 'townies' of Hebden Bridge. In these days before mass communication the hill top villages could be virtually isolated from events at a national level. News was slow to get through. Consequently valley folk enjoyed sharing a joke at the expense of their supposedly slow-witted hill top neighbours. The story went around that in the early stages of the war, during one of the great recruiting campaigns, an old lady from Blackshawhead went down to Hebden Bridge to do a bit of shopping, and returned to tell a neighbour that the streets were full of young fellows, "dressed in yella." "Why doesn't tha' know there's a war on?" asked her neighbour.

"Aye well," was the reply, "they've 'ad a fine day for it onyroad."

Nevertheless, humour could only be a temporary sticking plaster over the deep wounds that the war was inflicting by the end of 1915. There had been the disaster at Gallipoli and no sign of an end to the stalemate on the Western Front. The first use of poison gas in this sphere, by the Germans, had only intensified the inhuman aspect of the war. Meanwhile the casualties on all sides were mounting. Whereas no more than ten men with local connections had died by the end of 1914, by the end of 1915 a further thirty or so had been added to the list. This figure is an approximation for it relies totally on local press reports which, in turn, relied on information from the afflicted families.

Every one of these deaths was a tragedy, but the one that provides most shock impact is that of George Wilfred Robertshaw of Eton Street, Mytholmroyd. George enlisted with the 'Dukes' in July 1914. Formerly a member of Mytholmroyd Church Lads' Brigade, George was an apprentice moulder at Thomas Pickles and Sons, iron founders, prior to enlistment. All very straightforward, except that George was only fifteen years old when he enlisted, three years below the official minimum age required. By October 1914 he was fighting in France, was wounded in November, returned to the front and was killed in action on February 24th 1915, having by now reached the age of sixteen.

How could this have happened? In giving the news of his death the *Hebden Bridge Times*, somewhat apologetically commented as follows. "He was a big lad of his age and anyone would have taken him to be of full soldier age." Clearly this was enough to satisfy the enlistment officer. Deaths are inherent to war. Some are unavoidable; this one was not.

Pte G W Robertshaw DofW
Born 1899 Mytholmroyd
KIA 24 February 1915 aged 16

G.W. Robertshaw, a Mytholmroyd boy – only 16 at his death.

CHAPTER 8 – SOLDIERS' STORIES - 1915

Until the Defence of the Realm Act, the government Press Bureau sought to control the flow of war news. The old saying that 'the first casualty of war is truth' was amply demonstrated in August and September 1914 when the Press Bureau released heavily doctored reports of the early fighting at Mons and Le Cateau, playing down British reverses and emphasising British gallantry. The reports were printed in the national papers and picked up by the local press. Journalists were banned from entering the front line areas. As a result, genuine news as to the progress of the war was hard to come by, even news of casualties. There was, however, a loophole. Letters home from soldiers often contained a surprising amount of detail about conditions on the front line, even though censored by officers. Local newspapers encouraged recipients to allow them to publish such letters, often paying them for the privilege. A public hungry for news eagerly devoured these letters and the often graphic descriptions they contained.

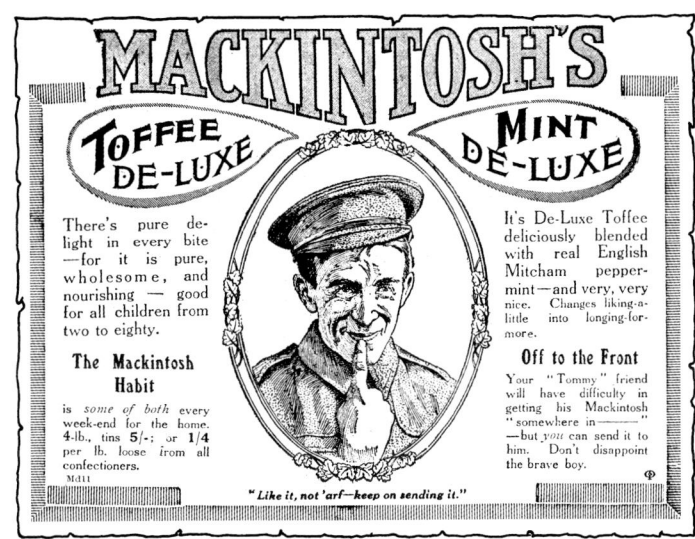

Could a toffee 'sweeten' life in the trenches?

In January 1915 the *Hebden Bridge Times* published a letter from Lieutenant J. C. Hoyle, the son of wholesale clothing manufacturer, J.JB. Hoyle. His report emphasised the miserable conditions under which both sides laboured across a landscape of ruined villages and flooded fields. The latter was partly a result of shelling destroying the drainage systems, but also a ploy used by both sides to make life more difficult for each other. Lieutenant Hoyle described how the Germans had diverted a stream to flow into the British trenches. The task of bailing out dug-outs full of stinking mud and water was made even more difficult by the attentions of German snipers who made a point of targeting the officers.

Humour was one way of coping with such miserable conditions and the following parody of *My Little Grey Home in the West*, widely circulating amongst the British 'Tommies' in Flanders and printed in the *Hebden Bridge Times* in January 1915, clearly reveals some bitter realities in a seemingly light-hearted ditty.

A Little Wet Home in a Trench
I've a little wet home in a trench,
Where the rainstorms continually drench,
There's a dead cow close by,
With her hoofs towards the sky,
And she gives off a beautiful stench.
Underneath in the place of a floor,
There's a mess of wet mud and some straw,
And the Jack Johnsons tear,
Through the rain sodden air,
O'er my little wet home in the trench.
There are snipers who keep on the go,
So you must keep your napper down low,
And their star shells at night,
Make a deuce of a light,
Which causes the language to flow.
Then bully and biscuits we chew,
For it's days since we tasted a stew,
But with shells dropping there,
There's no place to compare
With my little wet home in the trench.

Communications such as these from the Western Front cannot have brought much joy to the organisers of the great recruiting campaigns going on in Hebden Bridge and district at the time. Even the breezy letter from Private H. Sutcliffe of Hebden Bridge, in July 1915, stating how much he was enjoying trench life, contained the possibly mixed message that the 'Jack Johnson' shells lobbed over by the Germans created craters that would, "make fine swimming baths." Earlier in the year, however, news of a much more sinister threat than these huge German shells was filtering through to the columns of the *Hebden Bridge Times* – reports that the Germans were using poison gas.

During the Second Battle of Ypres (April 22nd to May 25th 1915) poison gas was used by the Germans for the first time on the Western Front. Hill 60 was a focal point in the fighting, and the local 2nd West Riding Regiment (Duke of Wellington's) was heavily involved. Private William Albert Thomas, formerly of Birchfield Villas in Hebden Bridge, went missing on May 4th and it was suspected that he had been the victim of, "noxious gas." It was confirmed the following month that he had been gassed by the, "fiendish asphyxiating fumes used by the Germans." Other local victims of the notorious Hill 60 were Privates Albert Howarth of Mytholmroyd and John Kershaw of Charlestown.

The Cloth Hall at Ypres in 1917 – somewhat different from the image on Albert Ogden's hankie.
Courtesy of Australia War Memorial E00717

Nor did news published in the local press from the Turkish Front offer much joy for those who were trying to persuade young men to don uniform. In September 1915 Private Willie Hughes, of Hebden Bridge, gave a graphic account of his participation in a bayonet charge at Gallipoli. In a hail of shrapnel and machine gunfire (which he described as 'hell'), he was only saved from death by a pocket book in his top pocket which took the full force of a bullet which embedded itself there. And so by mere chance the life of Willie Hughes was preserved, a man who was later to become the proud father of the future Poet Laureate, Ted Hughes. Later in his letter, Willie made no bones about the fact that after four days of hard fighting, with virtually no sleep, he fervently hoped that the rumours of his brigade being withdrawn from the Peninsula would turn out to be true. This says much about the terrible reputation of Gallipoli, as Willie Hughes was a courageous man who was later to win a Distinguished Conduct Medal for his bravery. A fellow member of the Lancashire Fusiliers, Private Jack Nicholson, was also writing home in September 1915 to his brother George in Hebden Bridge. He confirmed Willie Hughes' views of Gallipoli in the following comment, "I did not think that the war was as bad as this. It would open a lot of people's daylights to just hear the guns speak as they do out here."

A souvenir hankie brought home by Albert Ogden of Carr Farm, Mytholmroyd.
Courtesy of the Ogden family

Chapter 8 – Soldiers' Stories – 1915

> **A NATURE LOVER IN FRANCE**
> Whereas the letters home from most soldiers tended to concentrate on life in the trenches, a letter from Herbert Harwood, of Pecket Well, revealed a man with an observant eye for rural life in France. He wrote of the long, straight roads with carefully pruned trees on either side. He regarded the agricultural implements as out of date, but was fascinated by the way dogs were put to work – harnessed to light carts or running round a wheel to rotate a churn – treatment that would be, "considered cruel in England." Clearly a lover of the natural world, Herbert listed the birds he had seen, including sparrowhawk, merlin and kestrel. Birds in general flew about the trenches, "unmindful of the tremendous noise of the guns." One dawn, he spotted a fox in 'no-man's land.'

'Zam-Buk,' cured just about anything.

It seems extraordinary that, on the one hand, the War Office was in the midst of a huge recruiting campaign whilst, on the other hand, no censorship was imposed on the letters home that were revealing the truly horrific fighting conditions under which the soldiers laboured. Nevertheless, although recruitment in Hebden Bridge and district was seemingly falling below expectations in 1915, men continued to come forward. Perhaps the lure of adventure and glory still beckoned, for not all reports from the battlefields were negative. In February 1915, Private Sutcliffe Helliwell of Hebden Bridge, a reservist with the King's Liverpool Regiment, was home on leave and gave a stirring account of the fighting on the River Aisne in 1914. Having been hit in the shoulder, he still returned to the line of fire to help carry a wounded officer to safety. Not content with this, he returned again to carry a wounded private to the British trenches, all the while under heavy German fire which resulted in Private Helliwell receiving a leg wound. For these actions he had been recommended for a Distinguished Conduct Medal.

Then again, a series of jaunty letters in the *Hebden Bridge Times*, under the pen name of 'HEBDEN,' made light of the conditions in Flanders. One of the writer's first contributions, in May 1915, describes how the mansion in which he and his mates were billeted was struck by a German shell and compares the subsequent evacuation of the building as something like a scene from the Keystone Cops. Later, in the midst of death, the plight of three abandoned kittens becomes of overwhelming importance to his company, which adopts them. "They now ride proudly on the packs of three men, completely indifferent to the whistle of occasional bullets."

> Another light-hearted missive from 'HEBDEN' appeared in June 1915 under the heading of 'FURNISHING ON THE EASY HIRE SYSTEM.' It describes the building of a dug-out in an orchard, using mainly stolen timber, carpets etc. This provoked a furious argument between the 'Tommies' and a farmer over the ownership of a chair, a row which 'HEBDEN' portrays in true Dickensian style. "The brief simplicity of our retort may have been prompted by his obvious insinuation against our innocence, or it may have been due to a complete and humiliating failure to grasp the full purport of the linguistic torrent, ably supported by wild gesticulations, that he poured out."

It could only have been a remarkable man who could send such letters whilst enduring trench warfare conditions, and indeed he was. 'HEBDEN' was Edmund L. Ashworth, aged 29, the youngest son of Alice and Handley Ashworth of Sandy Gate, Hebden Bridge. A talented all-round sportsman and a highly

> *his former cricket prowess made him a top class grenade thrower*

popular teacher, first at Stubbings School in Hebden Bridge and later at Holy Trinity School in Halifax, Edmund was a territorial with the Duke of Wellington's Regiment. He was in uniform in August 1914, and after training his battalion arrived in France in April 1915 to be positioned near Ypres. Edmund was an excellent soldier, quickly becoming a Lance-Corporal, and his former cricket prowess made him a top class grenade thrower.

As 'HEBDEN' he sent another long dispatch to the *Hebden Bridge Times* in August 1915, making ironic references to officers, propaganda and the backroom boys, but at the same time referring to the local canal (which was being bitterly fought over) as an angler's paradise. He took care, however, not to portray the war as one big joke, for he could use language that was as raw as the situation demanded. "It is no picnic up there, as the sandbags red with blood and the stinking bodies that strew the neighbouring ground both testify."

The reality of this was brought home to Edmund's family when the news came through that he had been shot and killed by a German sniper, early on the morning of December 13th 1915, just as he had finished giving out rations to his section. The high regard in which he was held is demonstrated by the fact he had just been recommended to receive a commission and this had been approved.[1]

If Edmund L. Ashworth had injected a lighter tone into life at the front with his jaunty

**Edmund L. Ashworth;
a remarkable man in every way.**

letters home, then his death seemed to extinguish it. As 1915 drew to a close, news came through of the death of John Henry Greenwood of Calder Bank, Hebden Bridge, killed whilst on sentry duty on December 4th. A soldier in the Coldstream Guards, his last letter home (never posted but forwarded to his parents by a comrade) contained a bleak appraisal of the life he was leading. "It is a monstrous life of hardships and trials, and no one can realise, only those who witness it."

Early in 1916 came an incident that brought home to the locality, as never before, the tragic loss of young life in this war. Most soldiers died on the battlefield, or in hospitals abroad, and they were buried overseas. There was usually a memorial service at home, but without a proper funeral there was perhaps some distancing of these local fallen men from

---

1 More information about Edmund L. Ashworth can be found in *Hebden Bridge – A Sense of Belonging by Paul Barker*, pages 85-94, published by Frances Lincoln Limited. Paul's wife, Sally, is a great-niece of Edmund L. Ashworth.

the local population, with the exception of their relatives of course. However, a few men lost their lives without ever leaving the country, sometimes in curious circumstances. In July 1915 for example, a Private Pickles, serving with the Royal Scots Fusiliers, died from the effects of banging his head on the concrete floor of his barracks after being attacked by a fellow soldier. Again, Private George Harold Clegg of the King's Royal Rifles, one of a batch of the local Church Lads' Brigade who left Mytholmroyd in October 1914, died of illness in Woolwich Hospital in April 1915.

However, on January 10th 1916 Private Wilfred Uttley, Royal Fusiliers, died in Leicester Hospital of wounds received in battle and was brought home for burial at Heptonstall Slack Baptist Church on January 15th 1916. Wilfred Uttley was the first Hebden Bridge soldier to be given a local burial after having died of wounds received in combat and his story seems to have touched a raw nerve in the district. Wilfred Uttley was the son of Mr and Mrs Mitchell Uttley of 3 Beechwood View, Charlestown. A teacher and scholar at Broadstone Baptist Church and Sunday School, Wilfred was also a member of the choir and a good violinist. He worked at the firm of H. Ashworth and Co., shuttle makers of Hebden Bridge, and also helped his father out at Beechwood Nursery, a gardening business. In every respect Wilfred seems to have been a worthy and promising young man.

In May 1915, aged only nineteen, he enlisted, and was sent to France in November. After only two weeks there, and on his first visit to the firing line, he was seriously wounded by shrapnel, on November 26th. The doctors held out no hope for him and he was transferred to Leicester Hospital on Christmas Day. The parental visits to him were harrowing. This once bright and active young man could no longer speak, although his parents elicited a faint smile of recognition from his pale features.

The funeral of Wilfred Uttley, on January 15th 1916, seems to have released an outpouring of pent up grief in Hebden Bridge. According to the *Hebden Bridge Times*, thousands lined the streets to watch the coffin pass by on a gun carriage draped with the Union Jack. The parade, led by the local brass band, contained local councillors, magistrates, scouts, guides, fellow soldiers and representatives of virtually every local body and association. It was as if the town was in collective mourning, not just for Wilfred but for every local man who had lost his life in this war since August 1914. Mingled with the mourning there was probably also the silent acceptance that Wilfred would not be the last.

Wilfred Uttley; a popular young man of promise.
Courtesy of Keith Stansfield

The solemn funeral cortege of Wilfred Uttley.
Courtesy of Keith Stansfield

Hebden Bridge seems to have come to a standstill on the afternoon of the funeral. Many of the watchers would have heard of soldiers losing their lives overseas, but here was death at close quarters. This was a different perspective of war from that propounded by the rhetoric of the government recruiters – 'King and country,' 'glory and honour.' This was the grim reality of grieving relatives following a coffin containing the body of a young man known and liked by many of the onlookers. Wilfred Uttley, aged nineteen and barely out of his boyhood, the tragic waste of a promising future and something that was being replicated far and wide. The Reverend E.G. Thomas, in his address at Heptonstall Slack Baptist Chapel, made no bones about his views. He railed against the industrial nature of modern warfare, describing as horrible and diabolical, "the ingenious devices for slaying men." Referring to the youthfulness of Wilfred Uttley, he condemned the war as, "a slaughter of the innocents." Finally he asked this question. "Should it be that the best of our young men are intended as mere food for powder and shrapnel?" The answer was to be 'yes,' and in ever increasing numbers.

In Memoriam.

Private Wilfred Uttley,

19TH BATTALION
ROYAL FUSILIERS,

Died at Leicester on January 10th, 1916,
of Wounds received in France
on November 26th, 1915.

Interred at Heptonstall Slack, January 15th, 1916.

LEAD, kindly Light, amid the encircling gloom,
    Lead Thou me on ;
The night is dark, and I am far from home ;
    Lead Thou me on.
Keep Thou my feet ; I do not ask to see
The distant scene—one step enough for me.

I was not ever thus, nor prayed that Thou
    Shouldst lead me on ;
I loved to choose and see my path, but now
    Lead Thou me on ;
I loved the garish day, and, spite of fears,
Pride ruled my will : remember not past years.

So long Thy power hath blessed me, sure it still
    Will lead me on
O'er moor and fen, o'er crag and torrent, till
    The night is gone,
And with the morn those angel faces smile
Which I have loved long since and lost awhile.

Wilfred's death caused a profound shock to the community.
Courtesy of Keith Stansfield

CHAPTER 9 – TODMORDEN'S TRAGEDY – GALLIPOLI

The narrow stretch of water known as the Dardanelles Straits, linking the Mediterranean to the Black Sea, and overlooked by the rugged Gallipoli Peninsula, was merely a name on the map for the majority of the citizens of the Calder Valley prior to 1914. However, the name 'Gallipoli' was to carry a particular resonance during the decades that followed the Great War, especially to the people of Todmorden. Whereas volunteers from much of the Calder Valley tended to turn their faces eastwards towards Halifax and the West Riding Regiment, the men of Todmorden tended to look westwards towards Rochdale and the Lancashire Fusiliers, a trend that spread itself into Eastwood and Charlestown, midway to Hebden Bridge but constituting a sort of 'no man's land' between the 'Toddites' and the 'Briggers.' The Sixth Battalion of the Lancashire Fusiliers was a territorial unit recruiting in Middleton, Rochdale and Todmorden. Two companies, about 200 men, were based in Todmorden under Captain (later Lieutenant Colonel) J.J. Gledhill and Captain (later Major) R.H. Barker. The former was a solicitor and Conservative member of the Town Council, whereas Captain Barker was the son of a local mill owner.

Captain (later Major) R.H. Barker.
J.A. Lee

Captain (later Lieutenant Colonel) J.J. Gledhill.
J.A. Lee

At the declaration of war, on August 4th 1914, all territorial units were mobilised and on August 7th the Todmorden men undertook the march to battalion headquarters at Rochdale, cheered off by a huge crowd. Territorial units had been initially raised for home defence, and as such had to specifically volunteer for foreign service. Only about half the Todmorden men did, but great recruiting speeches made at the Town Hall by Captains Gledhill and Barker aroused such enthusiasm that eager volunteers came forward to more than make up the numbers in the two Todmorden companies. These territorials, both old and new, were keen to show that they could be more than just 'weekend soldiers.' Not many months would pass before they would have to show their mettle.

After training at Turton, what was now known as the 1st/6th Battalion of the Lancashire Fusiliers arrived at Alexandria, Egypt, on September 26th 1914. More gruelling training followed in Egypt to acclimatise the men to the Eastern Mediterranean heat. If the men of Todmorden had to get used to Egypt, then some of their fellow soldiers from other parts of Lancashire had to get used to them. Lieutenant Norman Holden spent a night in a dug-out in the desert with some Todmorden men. He wrote in his diary, tongue in cheek, that he was now convinced that Todmorden was the best health resort in England and that he had now discovered, "the exact location of the Garden of Eden."[2] If Todmorden was akin to Paradise, then some of its menfolk were about to enter something approaching Hell.

Men of the 6th Battalion, Lancashire Fusiliers, leaving Todmorden Drill Hall August 7th 1914.

J.A. Lee

About to land at Gallipoli – little knowing what awaited them.

J.A. Lee

In the early evening of May 2nd 1915, the 6th Battalion of the Lancashire Fusiliers boarded the troop carrier *S.S. Nile* anchored off Alexandria. The ship arrived at Cape Helles on the Gallipoli Peninsula on the evening of May 4th, those on board for the most part probably unaware that their presence was a continuation of Winston Churchill's ambitious plan to capture Constantinople, knock Turkey out of the war and aid Britain's ally, Russia, from the south. This plan had been ongoing since February 1915, with little success and much bloodshed. The following morning the troops crowded into two small tenders, about 200 in each, and made a fairly uneventful landing.

There was a wait until dusk and then followed a five mile march to the front line trenches, accompanied by the constant sound of shell and gun fire. It must have been an unnerving experience for the 'unblooded' territorials as they began to pass corpses and dead horses, every so often flinging themselves to the ground as a bursting Turkish star shell illuminated the landscape. The Lancashire Fusiliers relieved the King's Own Scottish Borderers in the front line

---

2 Quotation taken from *The Gallipoli Oak* by Martin Dawson and Ian Purdy, page 5, published by Moonraker (2013), an excellent source for the Gallipoli Campaign.

trenches. The latter departed with grim faces and in a silence that perhaps spoke volumes. It was not until 3 a.m. on May 6th that the entire

Their noses were assailed with the terrible stench of corpses.

Battalion was settled into the trenches. Action was to come sooner than anyone had anticipated.

As dawn broke on May 6th, for those who took the risk of popping their heads above the parapet, the dispiriting sight which met their eyes was that of piles of Turkish and Scottish dead. Their noses were assailed with the terrible stench of corpses. News came down the line that at 11 a.m., having had little in the way of food and sleep, three companies of the 6th Battalion were to go 'over the top.' The officers were now struggling to ascertain either their own position or that of the enemy from the inadequate maps with which they had been issued.

The start was delayed, but at 11.30 a.m., with Todmorden men in the vanguard, D and C companies of the 6th Battalion Lancashire Fusiliers went 'over the top' with the object of capturing the village of Krithia and the hill of Achi Baba. Running over open ground they were met with a storm of machine gun fire, rifle fire and shrapnel. The initial aim of taking a ridge was achieved, but eight Todmorden men were killed (including seventeen year old Frank Barker of Elder Bank). Captain Gledhill was wounded in the arm and had to be dragged off the battlefield on his back in a two hour nightmare ordeal. Meanwhile Sergeant A. Hamer was winning the Distinguished Conduct Medal – the first honour of the war for a Todmorden man.

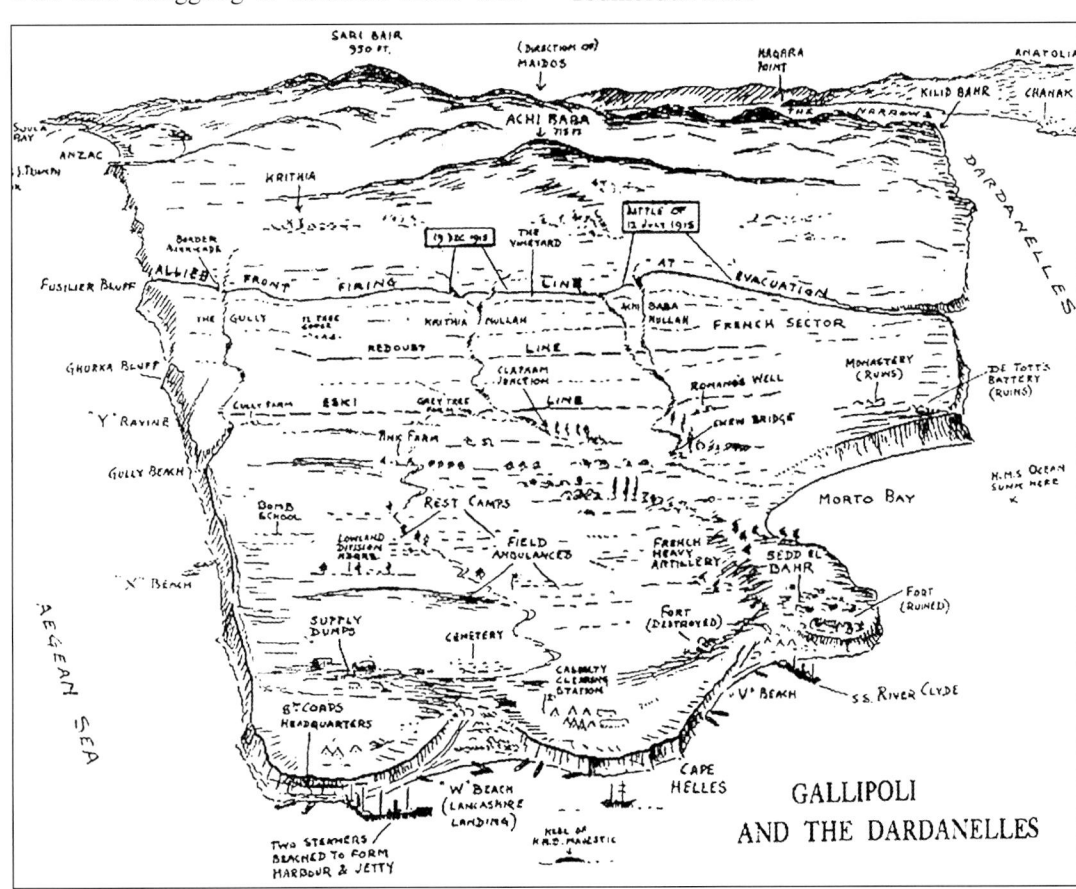

The congested battle zone where so many lives were lost.

Courtesy of Steve Wright

Eye witness accounts of this terrible engagement give a flavour of it. According to Private Arthur Howarth, a Todmorden fireman, "Some of our poor lads never got on top of the trench before they were shot dead. It was hell upon earth." (*The Gallipoli Oak*, p78). 'Bobbie' Johnson of Todmorden thought that he was making some progress when he received a stunning smack. "I looked round slowly to see my arm blown into a fantastic shape. A shell burst overhead and the shock made me deaf and speechless." (*The Gallipoli Oak*, p79) To make matters worse, little or no provision had been made for the shifting of the wounded. There were no field ambulances. Overworked stretcher bearers had to carry their loads for two or three miles down to base, and many of the seriously wounded did not survive this trip. This opening battle had been a baptism of fire for the untried territorials, but all reports commented on the magnificent performance of the 1st/6th Battalion, which had suffered casualties of 228 (killed, missing or wounded).

For the next few weeks the 1st/6th found themselves withdrawn to the second line where they were engaged in trench digging and road making duties. However, this was very far from being 'a safe number.' Operating at the tip of a narrow peninsula, the Allied forces were never out of range of Turkish fire power. Shelling was spasmodic but sniping was a constant problem. Ernest Law, from Todmorden, was a signaller, his job being to look after one or more field telephones and pass messages and instructions from the rear to the front and vice-versa. Amidst all the noise, the danger and squalor, Ernest still had the presence of mind to keep a diary.

Within this relatively quiet time, his entry for May 23rd 1915 describes a lucky escape when the Turks sent over some high explosive shells. When the smoke and dust had cleared, "I had a look around and found three large pieces of shell about one foot from where I sat."[3]

Ernest Law of Todmorden – an eye-witness to events.

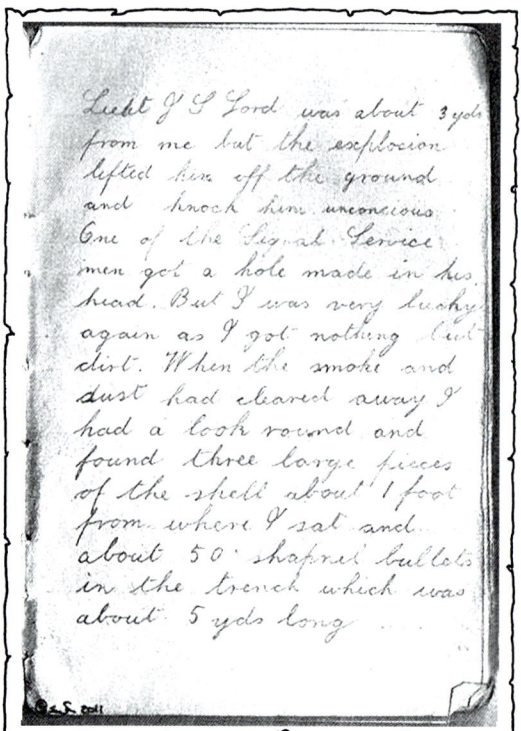

An extract from his diary.
Both images courtesy of Steve Wright

---

3 I am indebted to Steve Wright, of Todmorden, for allowing me to make use of this diary, written by his great-grandfather, Ernest Law.

Chapter 9 – Todmorden's Tragedy – Gallipoli

After the relative calm of a month's second line duties, the 1st/6th took part in their second bloody engagement, beginning on 4th June 1915, when another attempt to take Krithia, and the hill of Achi Baba beyond, was made. This time the Manchester Brigade was in the vanguard, and it was the job of the Lancashire Fusiliers to occupy and hold any trenches taken by the first wave. This was no easy job as the Turks attempted to retake their trenches. Fighting was heavy and often at close quarters, involving bayonet charges and hand to hand combat. Casualties were heavy on both sides and four Todmorden men won the Distinguished Conduct Medal on the first day – Company Sergeant Major Allister and Privates J.W. Child, R. Allen and H. Butterworth.

John William Child of Todmorden; winner of a D.C.M. at 17; killed at Krithia.

J.A. Lee

Amidst all the mayhem were two fifteen year old bugle boys who should have been kept in the rear but somehow had got into the trenches. They survived unharmed and, in fact, cried bitterly when they were escorted unwillingly back to base.

Meanwhile 'hard news' was hard to come by back home, and Todmorden was awash with rumour. A severe problem arose from the fact that the heavy fighting resulted in many of the dead lying unrecovered, either in 'no-man's land' or behind enemy lines. The Army could only list these men as 'missing' as they could have been taken prisoner. In most cases they were dead, but families at home could face an agonising wait of perhaps months before this

---

it had cost ten casualties for every yard gained

---

was confirmed. Therefore it could be a mercy when a family was quickly informed about the fate of one of their 'missing' members by a comrade in the Battalion. Such was the case of eighteen year old Willie Sutcliffe of Gledhill Street, Todmorden. Corporal Blakeney, his section commander, wrote to his parents, "I think it is my duty to let you know how your brave son died." He went on to describe how 'Bill' was hit in the head by a machine gun bullet, dying almost instantly. This was a case when the body had to be left behind, and so Willie Sutcliffe would have been listed as 'missing.' No matter how heart breaking the news was for the Sutcliffe family, it was better than a long and anguished wait until the Army confirmed his death.[4]

At this point it was estimated by Lord Rochdale, the Commanding Officer of the 6th Battalion, that after four weeks on the Peninsula it had cost ten casualties for every yard gained. He was highly dissatisfied at the inaccuracy of the maps provided and the apparent lack of knowledge of generals and general staff with regard to enemy positions and the conditions under which the men laboured. Armed with these and other complaints he left for England to take up these matters with the government. Meanwhile, in late June, the Battalion took a welcome fortnight's rest on the Greek island of Imbros.

---

4 Willie Sutcliffe was the author's uncle. Willie's older brother, Leonard, was shot in the throat at Gallipoli but eventually recovered after a long stay in a Liverpool hospital. Willie's body was never recovered. His name is inscribed on the Centre Vale Memorial, Todmorden, and on the memorial at Cape Helles to the men who died at Gallipoli but have no known graves on the Peninsula.

The respite was welcome but far too brief. On August 7th 1915 the 6th Battalion took part in an attack on the Krithia Vineyard, as a diversion from a new landing that was being made further north at Suvla Bay. This was perhaps the worst ordeal of all.

> *The territorials were men who, two months earlier had not so much taken part in a skirmish. Those who had survived the May and June attacks could count themselves as veterans, but they were now about to be engaged in some of the heaviest fighting ever witnessed at Gallipoli.*

From the first attack on the Turkish front line trenches, 250 yards away, it was sheer carnage on both sides. The battle raged continuously for two days and the intervening night, with trenches taken, then lost in counter attacks and then taken again. The fighting was often at close quarters with bayonets and rifle butts, fought with a savage and almost inhuman ferocity. The Krithia Vineyard was won and held. The Lancashire Fusiliers and the East Lancashire Regiment won plaudits for their courage, and there were many instances of individual heroism, but the cost was heavy. One of those to fall was Company Sergeant John Mason, at 47 years-old one of the oldest Todmorden volunteers and a man who was almost a legend in the regiment. After his death, Captain Crossley wrote home to Mason's wife. "He was the finest man I have ever had under me and I would have trusted him with my own life….and the men would have followed him to hell." (*The Gallipoli Oak*, p132).

As the weary survivors of the attack were relieved from their front line positions, it was time to count the cost. Of the fifteen officers of the 6th Battalion, 8 had been killed and 6 wounded. Since arriving at Gallipoli, the Battalion (around 1000 strong) had lost 10 officers along with 120 non-commissioned officers and men. Later 29 more died and 26 were missing. The wounded had reached the appalling total of almost 800.[5] Sadly, this costly diversion from the Suvla Bay landings had achieved little more than stalemate.

Dysentery, jaundice and septic sores spread like wild fire in this confined area.

As if the fighting were not enough, the intense heat of summer, combined with insanitary conditions, resulted in so much disease that it was more effective in reducing the fighting strength of the 6th Battalion than Turkish bullets. Dysentery, jaundice and septic sores spread like wild fire in this confined area. The number of unburied corpses led to a constant stench and also resulted in polluted wells and a huge plague of flies. One of the sufferers, Charles Watkins, described conditions graphically. "It was a physical impossibility to eat anything in the daytime…..without spitting out at the same time the flies who insisted on hovering on your biscuits, your bully beef, crawling over your lips, your eyes, and searching every inch of your face." (*The Gallipoli Oak*, p143) Another

Company Sergeant Major John Mason, Lancashire Fusiliers; a hero to both his men and his commanding officer. A Todmorden man.

J.A. Lee

---

5 Figures taken from *Todmorden and the Great War, 1914-1918* by John A. Lee, page 43, published by Waddington & Sons, Todmorden, 1922.

source gave a colourful description of the flies as, "blue and green monsters, too lazy to fly or crawl away, and to kill fifty was but to invite five thousand to the funeral." (*Todmorden and the Great War,* p44) Even those who did not succumb to dysentery found diarrhoea a constant problem, resulting in men losing weight and becoming emaciated. It may have been little consolation, but clearly the Turks were suffering in the same way. The Turks had gained a bad reputation at home. In this respect it is interesting to note the comments of a Private Jones of the 6th Battalion. "Don't you believe what you hear about atrocities performed by the Turks. You can take it from me (and I have been here four months) that the Turks are a fair lot of fighters." (*The Gallipoli Oak,* p149)

> **HIDDEN KILLERS**
>
> *The First World War was notable in being the first war in which disease was not the main killer as opposed to weaponry. Nevertheless a range of infections did take their toll, some of the victims being as follows: - A. Greenwood, Bertrand Blackburn, T. Adams and Horace Smith. These all died of dysentery in areas where conditions were unusually hot and insanitary – Palestine, Mesopotamia and Salonika. H. Kilby died of heat in Mesopotamia. H. Booth was brought down by malaria and acute nephritis in Salonika.*
>
> *A range of other conditions could also prove to be fatal. Some of the unlucky victims were: - William Henry Thomas (trench feet), Thomas Greenwood (meningitis), J.H. Sunderland (pneumonia), E. Sunderland and J.H. Pickles (influenza). As if that were not enough, accidents could also play their part, as with Charles Helliwell of 2 Beechwood View, Hebden Bridge, who was accidentally drowned in Mesopotamia.*

These late summer months were an odd mixture of comparative quiet interspersed with bouts of violent activity. On many occasions Ernest Law's diary entry simply read, "Very quiet all day." The Lancashire Fusiliers were back at the point from which they had launched their first attack in May, but in spite of always being in range of the Turkish guns, Ernest Law recorded more than once that men were walking freely about on top. In contrast, it comes as somewhat of a shock to read his entry for another day recording that when the troops were coming out of the firing line, "One of them got his head clean blown off by one of the Turk's shells about three yards away from me." Scandalously, the number of courts martial increased greatly at this time, the offence almost always being that of falling asleep on sentry duty. Prison sentences were being imposed of between two and ten years. Lord Rochdale, back at Gallipoli, was absolutely incensed at this, arguing that the men were suffering from malnutrition and sheer physical exhaustion, not able to sleep properly even when off duty because they were constantly in range of the Turkish guns. His pleas for clemency were brushed aside by the overall commander of the expedition, Sir Ian Hamilton, who put it all down to 'slackness'.

With colder weather coming in November, the troops were relieved to see the sudden disappearance of the flies. It must have seemed to them, however, that they were fated to suffer something like 'the plagues of Egypt,' simply one thing after another. The wind veered to the north and brought with it freezing rainstorms. On November 15th the rain was so torrential that the front line trenches were flooded. The troops had no choice but to get out on top. To their relief they found the Turks in the same position, so for a time the war was suspended whilst two lines of shivering soldiers faced each other in mutual misery.

> *On November 26th a fierce storm struck bringing both rain and snow. Further north, around Sulva Bay, nineteen men of the 1st Battalion Lancashire Fusiliers froze to death and twenty were drowned. The storm lasted for four days and resulted in more than 10,000 sick and injured men being evacuated from the Peninsula.*

The 'top brass' had now decided to abandon the whole misguided enterprise and a total evacuation was planned. On December 19th the 6th Battalion launched an attack as a diversion from the initial phase of the evacuation which was beginning further north. Three days of heavy fighting followed with more losses for the 6th, losses that were all the more tragic in that the end was agonisingly close, albeit unknown to the soldiers. Ernest Law recorded the experience in his diary, and in a touch of the macabre humour of the trenches he described the firing of the British guns from the ships anchored in the bay as, "sending the Turks iron rations." The 6th Battalion was relieved on December 24th by the 8th Manchester Regiment. Quite suddenly, on December 27th, the men of the 6th were evacuated. They gathered on the beach at dead of night, not yet fully out of danger as every ten minutes a high calibre Turkish shell screamed over and plunged into the hillside behind them. The Turks were not going to let the Lancashire Fusiliers go without replicating the 'welcome' they had received in early May. At last, however, they were out to sea and as a pink dawn rose over Gallipoli many men stood on deck, alone with their thoughts as they watched the Peninsula recede into the distance. The war was not over for them. They went on to fight in Sinai, and in March 1917 the 6th Battalion arrived in France where it took part in the terrible Battle of Passchendaele of that year.

Seventy-three local men never returned from Gallipoli. At least three hailed from Hebden Bridge, but the vast majority were Todmorden men. This was a significant number in terms of the size of the borough and the relatively concentrated period of fighting. The number includes men from other battalions of the Lancashire Fusiliers, and from other regiments. Of course there were many more wounded. Of the eight Distinguished Conduct Medals won at Gallipoli by the 6th Battalion Lancashire Fusiliers, six went to Todmorden men of 'C' and 'D' Companies. In the carnage of Gallipoli, the bodies of some of the 73 local men were either never recovered or could not be identified. Their names are engraved on the Helles Memorial.

With regard to the Calder Valley, Gallipoli was not an entirely Todmorden affair. The previous chapter has already referred to two Hebden Bridge men, Privates Willie Hughes and Jack Nicholson, who both fought there as members of the Lancashire Fusiliers. There must have been others. A problem arises when considering the 'no-man's land' of Charlestown and Eastwood. Recruits from this area tended to look towards Todmorden and the Lancashire Fusiliers. Of twelve who enlisted in August and September 1914, ten joined this regiment. James Lawrence, Wilson Butterworth and Arthur Tamblin lost their lives at Gallipoli; Frank Carling in France. Their names were inscribed on the Centre Vale Memorial in Todmorden, but were they 'Toddites' or 'Briggers'? In fact, as they hailed from Charlestown, part of the extensive rural area of Blackshawhead, they can be classed as Hebden Bridge men.

At least one Hebden Bridge man appears on this scene in Egypt just prior to Gallipoli :- Harold Barlow, third from left.

Courtesy of Peter Robertshaw

Chapter 9 – Todmorden's Tragedy – Gallipoli

The Carling family made a notable contribution to the war effort. Frank and Robert, both territorials, were sixteen at the outbreak of war, but less than one year later they were fighting at Gallipoli with the Lancashire Fusiliers. Both were wounded in June 1915. Meanwhile, their father, Arthur Carling, was playing his part in the Dardanelles Expedition with the Manchester Regiment. He went on to fight in France, where he was severely wounded in the head and lost the sight in one eye. Sadly, his son Frank was killed in action in France. His other soldier son, Robert, remained at Gallipoli to the bitter end and was later wounded once again, in France.[6]

Frank Carling – killed in France.
Eastwood Album

Robert Carling – wounded.
Eastwood Album

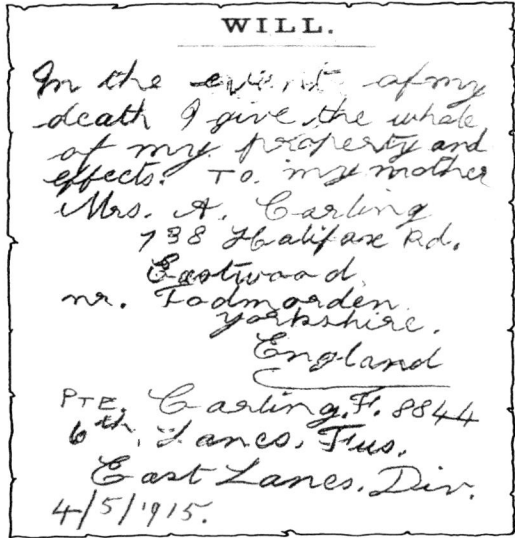

These hasty 'last minute wills' were not uncommon.

Nevertheless it was Todmorden which felt the weight and burden of the name 'Gallipoli,' a name branded into its consciousness for the rest of the war and for many years afterwards. So much so that Major R.H. Barker, who had seen so much sacrifice at Gallipoli, stood for the Sowerby Division in the general election of December 1918 as a candidate for the Association of Discharged Sailors and Soldiers. Several similar candidates stood in other parts of the country, but Major Barker was the only successful one. His demand for fair treatment for former servicemen appealed to the radical local spirit. Again, no doubt the memory of Gallipoli was to the forefront when, after the war, an impressive £13,500 was raised in Todmorden in one month in order to create a worthy memorial to the fallen of the borough.

---

6 Information and photographs concerning the Carling family taken from Eastwood Congregational Church and School: Young People's Society, Comforts Committee, Historical Album 1914-1920. Hebden Bridge Local History Archive.

The Garden of Remembrance was opened at Centre Vale Park on October 9th 1921. As well as statuary, the terrace wall was home to 24 tablets of Portland stone on which were inscribed the names of 659 men[7] of the borough of Todmorden who lost their lives in the conflict of 1914-1918, an impressive tribute which remains to this day. The emotions evoked by this memorial are perhaps best summed up by another tablet which simply states, "These are they who, being peaceable citizens of Todmorden, at the call of King and Country, and in defence of their Native Land, left all that was dear to them, endured hardship, faced danger, and finally passed out of the sight of Man by the path of Duty and Self-sacrifice, giving up their own lives that others may live in Freedom."

One of the most solemn events in Todmorden's history.
Courtesy of Bankfield Museum

Todmorden's magnificent memorial to its dead.
Louise Thomas

The inscription echoed those found on the scrolls presented to the families of the fallen.
Louise Thomas

---

7 Recent research by Todmorden man, Bryan Earnshaw, has now pushed the total up to 726, with a 'closing date' of 1921. These were men with any connection at all with Todmorden.

CHAPTER 10 – CONSCRIPTION

By 1915 it had become abundantly clear that, despite the seemingly insatiable demands of the army for more and more men, the 'rush to the front' was over. Those who had wanted to go had gone as volunteers. The huge recruiting drives were not now producing the desired numbers. The eligible men left, probably influenced in part by letters in the press which exposed the terrible realities of front line life, showed increasing reluctance to join up. The word 'conscription' hung heavily in the air.

> **SATURDAY NIGHT AT THE FRONT**
>
> *Louis Armstrong, of 46 Windsor Road, was one of the batch of 55 Hebden Bridge recruits who joined up in May 1915. Like many of them, he served in the Royal Fusiliers. He was well-known locally as a rugby player and a runner. No doubt he had enjoyed many a Saturday night in Hebden Bridge, but in a letter home, dated December 29th 1915, he left no-one with any illusions about the equivalent at the front. "Up to the waist in mud and water in the trenches. Five days without a shave or wash. Spent Saturday night having to stand-to with bayonet fixed, whilst the Germans, 100 yards away, were sweeping the parapet with machine gun fire." Sadly, this was his last letter home. Louis, aged 26, was killed in a shell burst early in January 1916.*

The most outspoken opponent of conscription was the Independent Labour Party, which had in any case opposed the war itself from the outset. In July 1915, at the monthly meeting of the Hebden Bridge Branch of the I.L.P., the following resolution was passed, "That this meeting declares its strongest opposition to compulsory military service, believing conscription in any form to be a violation of the principle of civic freedom." The resolution went on to describe conscription as, "a yoke which is one of the chief causes of Prussian militarism." The 'official' Labour Party had adopted a softer line to recruitment, but even so at a meeting in the Co-operative Hall, Luddenden Foot in December 1915, attended by around 100 delegates from trades unions and Labour organisations in the Sowerby Division, a protest resolution was passed in which conscription was described as militarism, "the defeat of which thousands of Englishmen are being called upon to sacrifice their lives."

This was swimming against the tide. That the game was up for voluntaryism had been shown by the results of a great recruiting meeting held at the Market Ground, Todmorden, on September 24th 1915, attended by a crowd of two to three thousand and supported by a band of the Lancashire Fusiliers. The plain argument of *fairness* was

Still the call for recruits came.

put forward. Why should some go and risk their lives on behalf of the nation whilst others stayed at home in safety and often in receipt of increased wages? The outcome was dispiriting for the organisers. The following week's enlistments in Todmorden barely exceeded the week's casualties. Nevertheless conscription was not a simple matter. It was a political 'hot potato' within the ranks of the coalition government which was running the war. The Conservatives were for it but the Liberal Prime Minister, Asquith, believed that it offended Liberal principles. In the end it fell upon the Secretary for War, Lord Derby, to try and implement a last ditch compromise to preserve a semblance of voluntaryism.

According to a national register published in September 1915, there were almost 5 million men of military age in Britain who were not in the forces. Of these, 1.6 million were 'starred' i.e. exempt from military service because they were engaged

---

Asquith stated that no married men would be called up until all eligible unmarried men had been taken.

---

in work of national importance. Lord Derby's scheme, introduced in November 1915, required a canvas of all eligible men to be completed by December 12th. Men were to be asked if they would 'attest,' i.e. enlist straight away or be willing to be called up later if needed. Khaki armlets with a red crown were to be given to those who had 'attested' and to medically discharged ex-soldiers. Those who would do neither were to be asked to give their reasons. Asquith stated that no married men would be called up until all eligible unmarried men had been taken. It was clear to all that the threat hidden in this scheme was that if it failed to produce the necessary men, conscription would follow.

The scheme entailed an enormous amount of work at local level and Civilian Recruiting Schemes were set up throughout the valley. It was envisaged that volunteer canvassers would visit 'unstarred' men in their own homes, but it was reckoned that there were 3,133 of these in Todmorden borough alone. When the Todmorden committee changed the procedure so that 'unstarred' men were invited to the Town Hall to fill in their cards, this turned out to be quicker and more productive, so that other local committees followed suit. At Hebden Bridge, for example, the Victoria Hall was used.

A HIGH STAKES 'DARE'

A trio of Hebden Bridge friends probably thought that it was just a bit of fun when they dared each other to join the army. The stakes were high, however, and the consequences were tragic. Edgar Helliwell and Frank Sunderland were killed, whilst Fred Greenwood was wounded, all in 1916.

Edgar Helliwell, one of the two who paid the full price for a light-hearted 'dare.'

Chapter 10 – Conscription

As a last ditch attempt to preserve voluntaryism in recruiting, Lord Derby's scheme was no more than 'smoke and mirrors,' simply a prelude to conscription. However, it did in theory give an idea of how many men were available (and willing) to be called upon. Early in 1916 a looming Military Service Bill was mentioned by Lord Derby in a letter to local councils. This sparked a vigorous response in some quarters, notably Hebden Bridge, where an epic and memorable meeting took place at the Co-operative Hall on Sunday, January 16th 1916, gleefully reported in the *Hebden Bridge Times* under the banner headline of 'UPROARIOUS CONDUCT AT HEBDEN BRIDGE.'

The meeting was officially an anti-conscription meeting held under the auspices of the local Trades and Labour Council but was hi-jacked from the start. As soon as the doors were unlocked a large body of armleted men, clearly 'attested,' charged in and were followed by two local recruiting officers, Mr J.H. Clegg and Mr Lobley. There was loud cheering as these two took the platform and the mob seized the first objective of the attack – the piano. An armleted man then began to play, first the National Anthem, followed by 'Tipperary' and other popular songs, all accompanied by loud singing. The rowdiness ceased long enough for recruiting officer Clegg to protest against an anti-conscription meeting taking place in Hebden Bridge and asking those present to vote on the matter.

Meanwhile, the official anti-conscription speakers, Mr J.W. Crowther (Chairman) and Mr Dawson, attempted to wrest control of the platform and oppose the vote. This, however, went ahead, resulting in an overwhelming

---

whenever Crowther tried to speak the piano struck up again accompanied by singing and 'cat-calls.'

---

majority against the holding of an anti-conscription meeting. A farcical situation then ensued with both Clegg and Crowther verbally slogging it out on the platform, Clegg pushing the patriotic line in favour of conscription whilst Crowther argued for the freedom of the individual to choose. This was a rather one-sided battle in that whenever Crowther tried to speak the piano struck up again accompanied by singing and 'cat-calls.'

In the end Crowther left the platform, approached the pianist and asked him to desist. His refusal led to a wrestling match for

The Co-operative Hall, Hebden Bridge, scene of rowdy meetings in 1916 and 1917.
Courtesy of Pennine Horizons

possession of the piano lid whilst a threatening crowd gathered round. Peace was abruptly restored, however, when the caretaker marched forward, shut the lid and locked up the piano. Some semblance of order was restored and the meeting ground to a halt, but not before Crowther and an angry young man had almost come to blows.

> *The reverberations from the anti-conscription meeting continued for some weeks. A letter from Mr J.W. Crowther appeared in the local press the following Friday protesting against the appearance at the meeting of recruiting officer, J.H. Clegg. A vigorous riposte from the latter came a week later. Clegg described the meeting as being organised by the 'Local Society for the Propagation of Funkers' (i.e. cowards). He also asserted that inconsistent rubbish had come from the Labour leaders on the platform and that conscription was now an absolute necessity.*

Clearly conscription was an issue which was producing much heated debate at this time, but the end product had much less impact than either the pro or anti-conscription lobbies expected. The Military Service Act of January 27th 1916 declared that all unmarried men ('attested' or not), between the ages of 19 and 41, would be deemed as having enlisted by March 2nd 1916. The act was extended on May 25th to married men also, with the lower age limit dropping to 18. A further act, in 1918, would raise the maximum age to 50, but no men in this older age group were asked to serve at the battle front.

The demand for fairness was satisfied by the Military Service Acts, for there was a general belief that there were hundreds of thousands of 'slackers' about. In terms of military need, the acts were less effective. In the first place 'starred' men, those who were in occupations of national importance (mainly munitions) were exempt from conscription. These numbered 1,433,827 in 1916, (figure taken from www.1914-1918.net/Long,longTrail). In addition many men, 'attested' or otherwise, were relying on a part of the act which, with typically British compromise, allowed men to apply for exemption from conscription on a range of grounds – occupation; ill-health; domestic circumstances and conscience.

The result nationally of this 'mish-mash' was that around three-quarters of a million men claimed exemption on one ground or another, in addition to the roughly one and a half million

> *"military conscription added little if anything to the effective sum of our war efforts."*

'starred' men. At a local level, for example, only around a half of the 3,133 men in the borough of Todmorden thought to be available for conscription actually 'attested.' Add to all this the number of men who simply failed to appear when called up (filling the courts), and those physically unfit to serve, it is little wonder that Auckland Geddes, Director of National Service 1917-1919, was later to state that, "military conscription added little if anything to the effective sum of our war efforts." In the first six months of conscription, the average rate of enlistment was less than a half of what it had been under voluntaryism. The crux of the matter was at the local level where Military Tribunals gave their verdicts on the applications for exemptions and provided fascinating material for the columns of local newspapers for many months to come.

CHAPTER 11 – THE RUSH TO THE BACK

The clamour for exemptions from conscription, as allowed in the Military Service Act of January 1916, finally confirmed that the 'rush to the front' of willing volunteers was nothing more than a fond memory. The problem now was how the local Military Tribunals were going to deal with the 'rush to the back' of the unwilling. The men sitting on these Tribunals were normally appointed by local councils. At Todmorden, for example, some were councillors and the rest were outside appointments. The original seven men contained a Justice of the Peace and three aldermen. In addition to the seven there was the Military Representative, W.A. Simpson-Hinchliffe. He performed this function at all the Military Tribunals in the Upper Calder Valley and his role was to put the case for the military as exemptions were being examined. Any decision could be submitted to an Appeal Tribunal.

The Military Tribunals usually sat two or three times a month and were exceptionally busy in the early months. At Todmorden about 100 exemption applications had been received in the month of January 1916. The men chosen to make the judgements were regarded as experienced, respected in the local community and possessing knowledge of local industry.

> *A.J.P. Taylor, in his English History 1914-1945, suggested that the Tribunals, "were composed of the elderly and retired, unsympathetic to all young men." J.A. Lee, writing about Todmorden shortly after the end of the war, took a less jaundiced view. He regarded the work of the local Tribunal as being of a delicate and responsible nature and credit was due, "to those who with conscientiousness and impartiality carried out this thankless task."*

There were many appeals on personal grounds, but the main battleground was between the needs of the employers on the one hand and the demands of the military on the other. Gone were the days when local employers had offered five or ten pounds to any of their employees who enlisted. Now, with many fit men already in the army, and facing a labour shortage, employers were desperate to keep the men who were left. Matters were not helped by the fact that the lists of certified occupations – those considered as of national importance – were constantly being changed, along with the ages at which people could claim exemption.

In such muddy waters it was easy for suspicions to be aroused. On February 18th 1916 an impassioned letter was printed in the *Hebden Bridge and District News* concerning the first sitting of the Todmorden Military Tribunal. It contrasted the decisions of this meeting – out of 86 appeals for exemption, only 10 refused – with the recent judgements of the Bradford Tribunal – 74 appeals; 51 absolutely refused; 21 postponed. To the writer

W.A. Simpson-Hinchliffe, the Military Representative on all the local Tribunals.
Courtesy of Pennine Horizons

it was clear that a particular class was over-represented on the Todmorden Tribunal which had adopted the text of, "business as usual," putting commercial considerations before the needs of the country.

The writer (who named him or herself 'ANTI-HUMBUG') then really warmed to the theme. The streets of Todmorden were apparently thronged with men who had no work to do but whose employers had had them 'starred' as being indispensable – young slackers who, "are moving heaven and earth to get on with their tin whistle polishing or hot cross bun baking." The writer concluded by demanding a new outside and independent Tribunal otherwise, "these young cowards will remain at large."

This was proof enough that if the idea of conscription had aroused strong emotions, then the composition and decisions of the Military Tribunals would equally arouse passions. The condemnation of the domination of the Tribunals by a particular class could be intensified if exemptions were being discussed not in terms of the indispensability of a particular employment, but in personal terms – domestic circumstances, ill-health or conscience. These were very subjective areas, fertile ground for accusations of favouritism or inconsistency.

The Gibson family gravestone shows brothers Arthur and Willie killed on the same day
Louise Thomas

EXCEPTIONAL FAMILIES – THE GIBSONS

Mr and Mrs Stott Gibson of Buttress Brink, Hebden Bridge, could take great pride in the fact that all of their six sons were involved in the war effort. Five of them – James, Ben, Arthur, Harry and Willie – joined five different army regiments, whilst Tom worked in munitions in Hartlepool. Sadly three of them did not survive the conflict. By a strange but unhappy coincidence, Arthur and Willie died on the same day, September 15th 1916, during heavy fighting on the Somme. Further misfortune befell the family when, on May 2nd 1917, Ben Gibson was killed by shellfire when going 'over the top' near Arras, France.

Yet a third brother killed – Ben Gibson.

Chapter 11 – The Rush To The Back

Three domestic cases brought before the Hebden Bridge Military Tribunal, in early March 1916, show how the margins were sometimes fine, perhaps incomprehensible to those not privy to the discussions. The first case was that of S. Helliwell of 19 Cliffe Street, Hebden Bridge, a bank clerk who claimed that his widowed mother could not do without him. A Tribunal could either accept an appeal, refuse it or grant a temporary exemption of a few months. S. Helliwell's appeal was refused. A similar fate awaited the appeal of Edgar Sutcliffe of Wood End, Hebden Bridge claiming to be the sole support of his widowed mother. However, he then went on to admit he had three married brothers and one sister, upon which the Chairman of the Tribunal declared that Sutcliffe's mother would be financially better off with him away from home. The third case; that of Fred Smith, a Mytholmroyd weaver, seemed on the face of it to be similar to the first two in that it

---

Ordinary working men were, no doubt, sometimes overawed by having to appear and speak before a panel of their 'betters.'

---

involved the support of a widowed mother. However, Fred Smith was granted a temporary exemption.

A judgment might depend entirely on the way a case was presented. In most domestic cases, men appealed on their own behalf. They had no representation. Ordinary working men were, no doubt, sometimes overawed by having to appear and speak before a panel of their 'betters.' Some were probably inarticulate and put forward a confused argument. Interestingly, Fred Smith's widowed mother appeared alongside him and spoke stoutly. The statement that her father had spent twenty-five years in the British Army certainly impressed the Military Representative, Simpson-Hinchliffe.

> *One of the most startling cases for the Hebden Bridge Tribunal came as late as August 1918. Wilbert Sutcliffe of 2 Slack Bottom, Heptonstall, claimed exemption on both domestic and indispensability grounds. As a tailor's cutter employed by Greenwood and Pickles at Bridge Mills, he was said to be continuously engaged on government contracts and was the only pattern cutter left at the firm. On the domestic side, this remarkable man had ten children (nine of them under twelve!); cultivated 300 yards of ground; and helped his father as a sexton at nights. Not much time for fighting then. Wilbert was given an exemption until February 1st 1919 and luckily the war was over by then.*

Those who sat on the Tribunals were not necessarily lacking compassion and friction could arise between them and the Military Representative who had a different agenda to follow. Quite a local storm was raised in April 1916 when the acting Chairman of the Hebden Bridge Military Tribunal, Joseph Clay, complained about the unfair treatment of 'medically unfit' claimants at the Medical Board, Halifax. He pinpointed the case of Herbert Varley, "which was the talk of the whole district." According to Clay, Varley was a delicate youth who had recently undergone an operation. He was in Halifax Infirmary and his treatment at the Medical Board had been, "of a most thoughtless and cruel nature." Presumably this Board was under strong military influence and Simpson-Hinchliffe may well have referred Varley (and others) to the Board to arbitrate on medical claims. Simpson-Hinchliffe was unrepentant, his only concession being to point out that under new arrangements such claimants could go to see a local army doctor rather than trail to Halifax.

> *The question of ill-health was one which gave the local Military Tribunals much trouble. Living and working conditions in the Upper Calder Valley were not conducive to good health in working class families anyway, but Tribunals were presented with many pitiful and harrowing stories from those seeking exemption because of ailing wives and sick children. A judgement on the genuineness of each story had to be made. This was not always easy, and after one particularly difficult session at the Todmorden Tribunal there was spontaneous laughter of sheer relief when the final claimant of the evening admitted that his wife and children were fit and healthy.*

On the other hand public opinion was not always on the side of those seeking exemption from conscription. At about the time of the Varley case, Simpson-Hinchliffe stated that he had received a great many anonymous letters denouncing the various ways in which single young men were trying to evade conscription. It is likely that this was a reopening of old wounds amongst those whose menfolk (particularly married ones) had already volunteered, and perhaps some had made the ultimate sacrifice. Simpson-Hinchliffe was eager to publicise this fact, and asked that names and addresses of these possible 'slackers' should be sent to him, and he in turn would guarantee anonymity to the informants.

On the industrial and commercial side of the coin, undoubtedly it was the one-man businesses which suffered most when it came to applying for exemptions from conscription, although admittedly John Selwyn Mitchell of Mytholmroyd, did not present a very convincing case. His argument that his barber's trade was indispensable to the community because of the strict rules of the military authorities concerning shaves and haircuts was given short shrift by the Hebden Bridge Military Tribunal in February 1916.

Similarly the Tribunal refused Herbert Midgley, a master butcher running his own business. On the other hand Selwyn Greenwood, a butcher and foreman slaughterman at the Hebden Bridge Co-operative Society, a substantial business, persuaded the Tribunal to accept his argument that he was, "in a skilled trade for the well-being of the country," and he was placed in a reserved occupation. One-man businesses could be hard hit if nobody could be found to take them over, especially if dependents were involved, and the prospects of reopening once the war was over were usually bleak. Cases of this kind were so numerous that in May 1916, in Todmorden, a protection society was formed known as the Todmorden Business Men's Military Service Protection Association.

Jack Shaw of Crown Street, Hebden Bridge, the proprietor of picture houses at this town and also at Luddenden Foot and Ripponden, found

---

he would have to close his three picture houses, meaning absolute ruin to himself and his mother and sister

---

himself virtually a one-man business after both his brother and his business partner had indicated that they intended to accept their 'call-up.' He himself now faced the same thing and in March 1916 he appealed to the Tribunal that he would have to close his three picture houses, meaning absolute ruin to himself and his mother and sister, both of whom were in poor health. The Chairman of the Tribunal could not be convinced that, "these picture palaces are essential to the nation at a time like this," and thought that recreation was not of national benefit. It was difficult for Shaw to counter this, although he did say that part of the takings also went to the Red Cross. He was given a temporary exemption until May 1st 1916, presumably to allow him some time to dispose of his businesses. This was a relatively easy decision for the kind of people who sat on such Tribunals. Dismissive of working class recreation, it was a decision which did not impinge on their own forms of recreation, for it was likely that none of them had ever set foot in a 'picture palace.'

Chapter 11 – The Rush To The Back

> *One of the favourite ploys of Simpson-Hinchliffe, the Military Representative, was to enquire as to whether a woman could do the job of a man who was claiming exemption. This was suggested to Joseph Lord at a sitting of the Todmorden Tribunal in March 1916. Lord both farmed and owned the Roebuck Inn at Portsmouth, Todmorden. He was claiming exemption for his son, John Lord, who had sole responsibility for running a farm of 68 acres with eight cows, four horses and twenty-two pigs. Joseph had also declared that he had a 40 year old daughter living at home, but reacted indignantly to Simpson-Hinchliffe's suggestion that she could be taught to milk cows.*
>
> *"What at her age? Anyway she has enough to do in the pub." Joseph's appeal was allowed.*

If domestic cases, one-man businesses and small farms presented enough problems to Military Tribunals, then the larger scale industrial and commercial arena was a minefield. The seemingly simple matter of reserved or certified occupations proved to be sometimes a 'grey' area. For one thing the government was constantly changing or amending the lists. Then there was the question of interpretation. Richard Baldwin, a sheet metal worker from Hebden Bridge, made the *guards* for lathes which produced munitions, and claimed exemption on these grounds. Was this really a certified occupation? Even Simpson-Hinchliffe did not know. The case was suspended until he could consult higher authority on this matter.

Gibson Bros. of Hebden Bridge posed a similar problem. Sam Gibson, one of the employers, appealed for exemptions for three men who made whipping machines for the *finishing* of hospital and military blankets, and this was government contract work. After the usual sparring over the question of using girls, which Mr Gibson declared to be unfeasible, once again the issue of certified occupations arose, and once again it fell upon Simpson-Hinchliffe to ascertain from the Ministry of Munitions as to whether these men should be 'starred' or not.

The much sought after reserved/certified occupation badge, which delayed or avoided conscription.

Courtesy of Pennine Horizons

It is likely then that the angry letter of denunciation by 'ANTI-HUMBUG' in relation to the first meeting of the Todmorden Military Tribunal was a little hasty in its judgements. The fact that out of 86 appeals for exemption only 10 were refused does not mean that the 76 were accepted. Many of these would have been given only temporary exemptions and some appeals suspended for further investigation. There is no doubt also that local industry was facing severe labour problems. Mr Harry Dixon, of the huge cotton manufacturing firm of Mons Mill, at Todmorden, stated to the Tribunal that out of a complement of 120 spinners, men and boys, 67 had enlisted and only eight spinning mules out of 36 were being worked. Nevertheless, his appeal to save yet another spinner, Dan Wood, from conscription, was only accepted for the next three months.

Hardship and Hope - Hebden Royd & Todmorden During The First World War (1914-1918)

Mons Mill, Todmorden had chronic labour shortages in these years.

Courtesy of Pennine Horizons

The accusation of 'ANTI-HUMBUG' that a particular class was dominating the Todmorden Military Tribunal and favouring its own people in the matter of exemptions is not really borne out by the evidence. It is true that powerful businessmen and manufacturers always made up a part of these Tribunals, and that men in a similar position were often facing them, making appeals on behalf of their own employees. They were not always successful however. One example was the case of Astin Bros. wholesales clothiers of Hangingroyd, Hebden Bridge, which came before the local Tribunal in March 1916. John Astin spoke on behalf of his son Fred, claiming that as the export manager he was absolutely indispensable to the business. However, the Chairman interpreted Fred's position as that of a bookkeeper rather than an export manager and Astin Bros. was given just a month to replace him. Fred remained in line for conscription.

On this occasion Simpson-Hinchliffe and the rest of the Tribunal were in accord. This was not the case a couple of months later. In May 1916 three prominent local clothing firms – R.B. Brown and Sons, C.W. Crowther Ltd. and William Gill and Sons – put in exemption appeals for three men with managerial responsibility. All three, Fred Harper Brown, John Henry Crowther and Ara Illingworth Gill were family members of the owners, and they were all granted absolute exemptions. The

He had gone as far as to do a little snooping around Hebden Bridge

Military Representative, Simpson-Hinchliffe, was himself an owner of mills at Cragg Vale, but he showed here that he would put the interests of the military before the commercial interests of people of his own class. He appealed against all three decisions to the Appeal Tribunal at Halifax. He had an ally there in the shape of Lieutenant Molesworth representing the Military. He had gone as far as to do a little snooping around Hebden Bridge and had discovered that the supposedly indispensable Fred Harper Brown spent much of his time in a café there. Molesworth had also been informed that Fred was not, "rushed for work." Having also picked up useful bits and pieces of information concerning John Henry Crowther and Ara Illingworth Gill, Lieutenant Molesworth managed to persuade the Halifax Appeal Tribunal that Simpson-Hinchliffe had been right in his appeal against the absolute exemptions.

The decision caused ructions at the next meeting of the Hebden Bridge Military Tribunal, in June 1916. The Chairman, Councillor George Atack, lambasted Mr Simpson-Hinchliffe, complaining that he had, "seen fit to appeal wholesale against the decisions of the Tribunal." He also protested that the members of the Halifax Appeal Tribunal could not know the circumstances of local trade and business as fully as the Hebden Bridge Tribunal and requested that the Local Government Board hand the decision back to this Tribunal. An unrepentant Simpson-Hinchliffe responded by stating that he was only trying to do his duty, "without fear or favour to anyone concerned." Simpson-Hinchliffe's argument was that he was against absolute exemptions, which could never be revoked, whereas temporary exemptions could respond to changing circumstances.

A postscript to the whole affair came not long afterwards when the Local Government Board informed the Hebden Bridge Tribunal that these cases could not be referred back to it. The letter ended on a sharp note, advising the Tribunal to, "get along with its business." As for Simpson-Hinchliffe he continued to show that he meant business when, in November 1916, he put an intimidating notice in the local press. In it he stated that, "the pressing need for men," meant that he and his advisory committees would be reviewing the cases of every local single and married man up to the age of thirty. All firms and factories would be visited, for it was his belief that men were still there whose claims for exemption had already been refused. In that case, employers *must* inform him or they would be breaking the Defence of the Realm Act. However, with regard to raising men, Simpson-Hinchliffe had problems in other quarters too. Issues were constantly arising as to those who could be termed the 'would nots' and those who regarded themselves as the 'could nots.' In other words 'Won't fight' or 'Can't fight.'

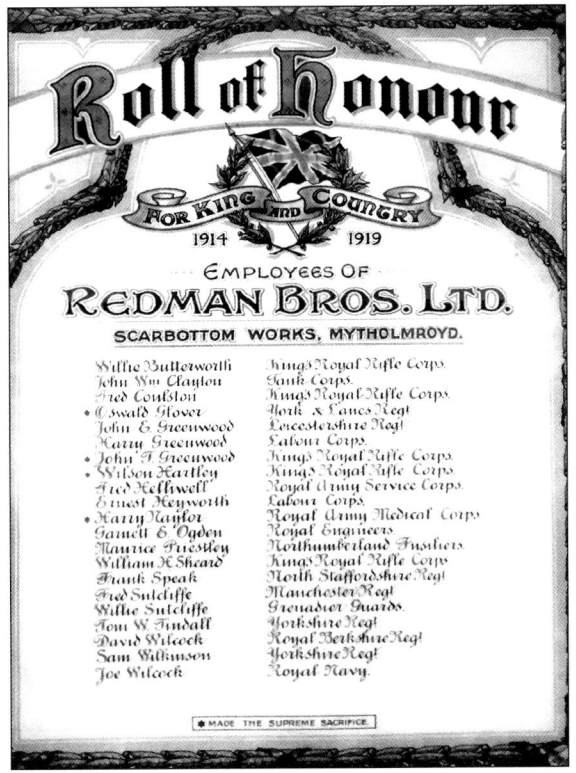

Local firms were keen to show their pride in 'their' men.

Courtesy of Bankfield Museum

CHAPTER 12 – WON'T FIGHT; CAN'T FIGHT

With the introduction of conscription, two groups emerged who caused particular problems to the military authorities – the 'would nots' and the 'could nots.' The former consisted of a disparate set of individuals who chose any means possible to avoid conscription. The latter formed a more coherent group, which chose to work within the system, but claimed exemption from conscription on grounds of conscience. The 'could nots' became generally known as the conscientious objectors, and they posed peculiarly difficult problems for the Military Tribunals. On the other hand, the 'would nots' by-passed such niceties as appearing before the Tribunals. They became a matter for the magistrates and police to deal with.

One early local example was Sam Cockcroft, a boot repairer of Bank Top, Mytholmroyd. A single man, he had simply refused to heed his call-up, and in March 1916 Sam appeared before the Todmorden Magistrates Court charged with being an absentee from His Majesty's Forces. He was fined forty shillings, and handed over to a military escort. Sam was nothing if not defiant, and had a few choice parting words for the magistrates which the *Hebden Bridge Times* discreetly reported as, "You can fine me forty *** pounds if you like."

Men sometimes went on the run to avoid military service, and the local magistrates had to deal with any who were apprehended in the district, even if they were not local men. In September 1916 rumours were circulating in the Bridge Lanes area of Hebden Bridge about a mysterious 'lodger' at the house of Mrs Schofield, of High Street, a 24 year old married woman whose husband was serving with the Forces. In spite of them moving about under

the couple were discovered in compromising circumstances.

the cover of darkness, it was known that the pair were jaunting off to Halifax every night. The suspicions of the police were aroused and a visit to 3 High Street was made at 12.40 a.m. Superintendent Peckitt had to threaten to use an iron bar to force entry before the door was opened, and the couple were discovered in compromising circumstances.

The mysterious 'lodger' turned out to be one Ellis Sutcliffe who, a few weeks earlier, had left Brooks' Chemical Works at Hipperholme without an exemption certificate, for his was not a reserved occupation. Sutcliffe was arrested and taken into military custody, whilst the local magistrates fined Mrs Schofield twenty shillings for concealing an army absentee.

A more pitiful case came before the Todmorden Magistrates Court shortly afterwards. William Jenkins, an iron turner of no fixed abode, was charged with 'tramping' to avoid military service. His wife, Mary Lavinia was charged with 'sleeping out.' Both had been collared by Constable Joseph Greenwood in Mytholmroyd. Jenkins was committed to custody until the military authorities collected him.

> With regard to William Jenkins' wife, ("a comely looking woman about 30"), the magistrates reacted in an interesting way. They listened intently to her story that she had been left alone and friendless since the age of 12, always living in lodgings, until meeting up with Jenkins. The magistrates were compassionate enough to provide her with enough money from the Poor Box to enable her to get out of the locality, to Colne, for she felt too ashamed to stay in a district where she was known.

These cases involved men who made no reference to conscience as a justification for evading military service, and it was relatively easy to deal with them. It was those who did bring conscience into the argument, as permitted under the first Military Service Act of January 1916, who posed difficulties for the Military Tribunals. According to the *Hebden Bridge and District News* for March 10th 1916, Hebden Bridge's first conscientious objector

> *Edward Sutcliffe and the Military Representative, Simpson-Hinchliffe, embarked upon a combined interrogation*

had appeared at the recent meeting of the local Tribunal. This was Thomas Clegg, a commercial clerk of 41 High Street, who appealed on personal grounds (both his parents were invalids) and on the basis of his long held moral and religious convictions that the taking of life was wrong. It seems likely that members of the Tribunal had prepared the ground beforehand for dealing with a case such as this, for one of its members, Edward Sutcliffe, and the Military Representative, Simpson-Hinchliffe, embarked upon a combined interrogation the substance of which was repeated on later occasions. The gist of it was to ask Clegg what he would do if a German threatened the life of his mother. Clegg's response that he would give his own life to save his mother's, but not engage in any violence, was dismissed as ridiculous by Sutcliffe. The Tribunal's deliberations ended in a decision to give Clegg an exemption until May 1st, but it was stressed that this was solely because of his father's health and not for any other consideration. Clegg later agreed to join up as long as his married elder brother was exempted – a bargain that was kept.

Two other cases of conscience which came before this particular Tribunal were those of Robert Dent Shackleton and Walter Lord. A citizen of Pecket Well, Shackleton had a

> *he avowed that the Bible forbade him from all forms of military service, including non-combatant*

supporting letter from the Reverend C.J. Hoskin in his claim to be a genuine

LOCAL CASUALTY LIST.

KILLED.
Pte. John Butterworth, 7, Prince Street, Todmorden.
Second Lieut. Harry Watson, Field House, Mytholmroyd.
Bombardier Walter Heaton, R.F.A., 2, Milner Royd, Luddenden Foot.

MISSING.
Pte. Arthur Calvert, Manchester Pals, Friths Terrace, Bacup Road, Todmorden.
Pte. Tom Holden, Square, Mytholmroyd.

PRISONERS IN GERMANY.
Pte. Frank Brooks, West Ridings, Chapel Street South, Walsden.
Pte. Tom Hopwood, Mayroyd, Hebden Bridge.

WOUNDED.
Gunner Fredk. Dehner, Bridge Gate, Hebden Bridge.
Pte. Frank Greenwood, Sherwood Foresters, West Laithe, Heptonstall.
Pte. Eric Clark, Highland Light Infantry, Hebden Bridge.
Pte. Sam Law, Melbourne Street, Hebden Bridge.
Rifleman George Hey, King's Royal Rifles, Mytholmroyd.
Pte. H. Sutcliffe, London Regiment, Hebden Bridge.
Pte. J. Bates, Duke of Wellington's, Luddenden Foot.
Rifleman Fred Helliwell, King's Royal Rifles, Mytholmroyd.
Rifleman John Heaton, K.R.R., Luddenden Foot.
Pte. Fred Greenwood, Seaforth Highlanders, Archway, Heptonstall.
Pte. Vincent O'Connor, Colden.
Gunner J. W. Lever, 5, Wood Street, Heptonstall.

Meanwhile the casualties were mounting abroad.

conscientious objector. His willingness to do non-combatant duty as an ambulanceman made it easy for the Tribunal to recommend him for non-military service. Walter Lord, of 17 Adelaide Street, provided a knottier problem. As a Christadelphian, he avowed that the Bible forbade him from all forms of military service, including non-combatant. He distributed a great deal of printed matter which the Chairman stated could not be properly read because of shortage of time, and he put to Lord the standard question concerning Germans and mothers. Lord gave a similar reply to that of Thomas Clegg and pressed for an absolute exemption. When he was told that he would only be granted exemption from combatant duty, Lord was distinctly unhappy and gave notice that he would appeal.

Chapter 12 – Won't Fight; Can't Fight

24th Royal Fusiliers Cap Badge

Such bookmarks were sad mementos for any family which had suffered a loss.

Perhaps the most contentious discussion at the Tribunal of March 1916 surrounded the claim for absolute exemption from Herbert Pickles of Wood End. He invoked the laws of God concerning the taking of life; fended off the Germans and mother scenario; but outraged the Tribunal by declaring that English rule was no better than German rule. One other problem for Pickles was that he was a member of no church, chapel or any religious group which could have given him its backing. It was no surprise then that he was exempted only from combatant service. There was a sequel to this in that Herbert Pickles appeared before the Todmorden Magistrates Court, in April 1916, and admitted not going when called upon under the Military Service Act. This now put him into the category of 'deserter,' and he was fined forty shillings and handed over to a military escort.

Conscientious objectors were generally unpopular. 'Conscies' was the rather derisory term applied to them and they were linked in the popular mind with pacifism. This in its turn suggested defeatism and an acceptance that the loss of so many young lives had been in vain. Herbert Pickles was not without support however. His arrest and imprisonment brought an angry response from the Halifax branch of the No-Conscription Fellowship. The branch secretary, Mr W.R. Stoker, protested through the medium of the press about the treatment of Pickles and other conscientious objectors throughout the land. The arrests were, "a positive disgrace to a professing Christian country like Britain." Stoker went on to demand, "the immediate release of all such martyrs."

This protest was followed up by a resolution passed at the Mytholmroyd branch of the No-Conscription Fellowship, strongly condemning the arrest of Pickles and others, "who have not broken the law." The Honorary Secretary, Mr H. Sutcliffe of Bank Bottom in Cragg Vale, pointed out that the Military Service Act (1916) provided for, "total exemption for conscientious objectors." Sutcliffe accused the military authorities of regarding the conscience clause as nothing more than a 'scrap of paper,' a clever allusion to the words used by the Kaiser in August 1914 in dismissing the treaty guaranteeing Belgium's neutrality.

> *Organisations stronger and more deeply rooted than the No-Conscription Fellowship were also pitching into the conscription argument. On the first Sunday of May 1916, the local branch of the Independent Labour Party held its traditional open-air meeting at Spa Lane Top, Cragg Vale. The visiting speaker, Mr A.W. Haycock of Manchester, described conscription as belonging to the type of German militarism which the allies were fighting to defeat.*

The trades unions were of the same mind as the Independent Labour Party concerning conscription. A meeting of the United Garment Workers' Union in Hebden Bridge, in May 1916, protested against the proposed extension of the Military Service Act as, "a conspiracy against…..the British people, more concerned with crushing British liberty and democracy than Prussian militarism." Nevertheless, both the trades union movement and the I.L.P. were cautious of drifting into the out-and-out pacifist camp as this might suggest that the working class sacrifice of lives had been all for nothing. In fact, the Peace Negotiations Committee was unable to get a room in the Hebden Bridge district to hold a conference in December 1916. Six months later the same committee did manage to hold a meeting on spare ground in Hebden Bridge. The principal speaker rejected the accusation of 'defeatism,' arguing that the country's war aims (protecting Belgium, France and Britain) had been achieved and so peace talks should begin.

MEANWHILE THE WAR GOES ON - A DARING ADVENTURER

Percy Tamblin of Ingle Dene, Charlestown, seemed to have stepped straight from the pages of one of the boys' adventure books of that era. Seemingly fearless of danger, he did not hesitate to dive into Foster Dam in 1912 to save a boy from drowning. Having taken on the unusual job of a warden at Melton Lunatic Asylum in Suffolk, he joined the Suffolk Regiment virtually at the outbreak of war. Whilst in France, and still barely twenty years old, in the middle of attack and under heavy fire, he dressed the wounds of two comrades shot in the head and carried one of them back to a dressing station. Later, during a night attack on German trenches, Percy found his officer wounded in 'no-man's land.' Regardless of his own safety, he persuaded another soldier to help him drag the officer to safety. For this he was recommended for the D.C.M. and promoted to Lance-Corporal. Sadly his record of helping others did not provide an 'adventure book' ending to the story, for he was killed in action in February 1916.

Percy Tamblin – the 'Daring Adventurer'.

Chapter 12 – Won't Fight; Can't Fight

Whatever the anti-conscription organisations said, however, it was the government which had the whip-hand in terms of the length of the war and who was to fight it. The key to the conscience clause was not that the Military Tribunals ignored it, but that it was virtually impossible to get total or absolute exemption on grounds of conscience. Generally conscientious objectors had their appeals totally dismissed or were granted some form of exemption, but only from combatant service. They had to agree to do some sort of work to help the war effort, either at home or engaging in such tasks as ambulance driving or stretcher bearing abroad. The real problem arose with the 'absolutists' – those who refused to do war work of any kind.

Towards the end of March 1916, the Mytholmroyd Military Tribunal was forced to confront this situation head-on. The first case may have lulled the Tribunal into a false sense of security, for it was very straightforward. Willie Sutcliffe's claim for exemption on grounds of conscience became laughable when he admitted that he was not a churchgoer and usually played cards on Sundays instead. No exemption of any kind was granted. The following cases, concerning seven men from Cragg Vale and Mytholmroyd, took the Tribunal aback. They stated that their convictions would not allow them to accept any verdict other than absolute exemption. Mytholmroyd, including Cragg Vale was an interesting hot-spot in terms of conscientious objectors. No less than eighteen have been identified, a figure way ahead of anywhere else in Calderdale in terms of the percentage of local males of military age. It was known that Mytholmroyd was a hotbed of socialism, therefore it is likely that the objections of these men were based on political as much as religious grounds.

> *The seven Mytholmroyd and Cragg Vale 'absolutists' – Riley Stocks, Joseph Meadowcroft, Verney Jowett, Herman Jowett, Ernest Walton, Arthur Riley and William Speak – predictably had their appeals for absolute exemption dismissed. Clearly this was going to be a case of the irresistible force meeting the immovable object, for by June all of them had been fined and handed over to a military escort after having failed summonses to attend Halifax barracks. The seven now faced a court martial for refusing military duties, the first one of its kind at Halifax, and the officials came to Halifax from the military authorities at York. The verdict was pronounced on June 16th 1916. The 'absolutists' were found guilty and sentenced to four months detention at Armley Prison, Leeds.*

How to deal with the 'absolutists' posed a difficult problem for the government. Nationally something like 17,500 men registered as conscientious objectors, but this counts only those who went through the official system. The majority of these agreed to do non-combatant work of various types, either ambulance and stretcher work abroad or

> *41 were transferred to France where they could have been shot for disobedience*

labouring on the Home Front on such tasks as road building. Labour camps for such purposes were run by the Home Office. Around 1,500 'absolutists' nationally refused all these options as contributing to the war effort. They were drafted into military units and imprisoned when they refused to obey the order of an officer. In 1916, during the early days of conscription, 41 were transferred to France where they could have been shot for disobedience. On the personal intervention of Asquith, they were brought back to Britain after one month. Imprisonment also carried its own risks and 71 pacifists died as a result of injuries sustained in prison.

DEATH OF A STRETCHER BEARER

Every death in a war is a tragedy in its own way, but it is particularly poignant when death comes to men who carry no arms and whose role is to save lives. One of these was James Currell of Garden Street, Hebden Bridge, a stretcher bearer. In December 1915 he won the Military Medal for his bravery in rescue work under shellfire. Writing home to his wife he modestly stated that, "It was my duty to help the poor wounded and gassed men." Sadly, his non-combatant status was not to save him. He was killed on July 10th 1916, leaving three children aged seven, four and two.

James Currell, stretcher bearer, killed on July 10th 1916.

Others who followed the little clutch of Mytholmroyd and Cragg Vale men who had tried to gain absolute exemptions in March 1916 fared no better. John Speak, a twister and overlooker, stated to the Hebden Bridge Tribunal that, "the war is wrong and in direct opposition to the teaching of Christ." He was allocated non-combatant duty and sent on his way to the accompaniment of the comment, "You will have to wear the nasty Conscience Corps Badge on your head," from one of the Tribunal. In December 1916 another Mytholmroyd conscientious objector, Harold Tabner Ashworth, was arrested for failing to join the colours, fined and handed over to a military escort.

Appeals on grounds of conscience were often couched in religious terms. Of the roughly 197 appeals made in Calderdale, around 130 quoted religious beliefs. Apart from one curious appeal based on vegetarianism, the rest embraced a more general morality or a belief in socialism.

Of the 197 appeals for exemption on grounds of conscience in Calderdale, 148 tribunal decisions are known. Four were granted total exemptions, but not on a basis of conscience. About half the rest were excused combatant service; the other half were totally refused. Most of the men who were excused combatant service performed works of national importance under the control of the Pelham Committee or their local Tribunal. Nine men served in the Friends' Ambulance Unit and a further one with the Friends' War Victims Relief. Thirty eight men were court-martialled.

If appeals on religious grounds were difficult to get through, then any whiff of politics spelt death to an appeal. Herbert Sutcliffe, another Mytholmroyder, claimed that as a member of both the Independent Labour Party and the No-Conscription Fellowship, he had always been opposed to all forms of militarism. He felt that his argument was moral, but the distinct impression left by the Tribunal was that it had even less time for this type of argument than it had for religious convictions, for Sutcliffe got a straight refusal. This fate was shared by Peter Bulcock of Cornholme when he stated to his local Tribunal that socialism and international brotherhood was *his* religion.

Elsewhere in the borough of Todmorden, a high profile case was being enacted early in 1917. Ernest Farrar B.A., the Headmaster of Todmorden Secondary School, had already been put in the Non-Combatant Corps, as a conscientious objector. It was reported on January 19th 1917 that he was one of 126 men in this Corps who had refused to handle munitions. As a result he had been arrested and sentenced to six months hard labour in Wormwood Scrubs. In March, however, the Central Appeal Tribunal accepted his stance as a genuine conscientious objector, and he spent the rest of his sentence on a Home Office work scheme. Later Farrar wrote to the governors of Todmorden Secondary School requesting his headship back if the school was understaffed. Although a group of parents sent a petition in favour of Farrar, the governors may have felt that their decision to vote seven to four against Farrar was more reflective of public opinion. They may or may not have been influenced by a letter from a parent saying that she would remove her children from the school if Farrar was reinstated.

> Sam Schofield, a tripe dresser from Walsden, chose an interesting ploy to avoid the call to arms. Apparently he had 'attested' in December 1916 on condition that he could join the Royal Army Medical Corps when the time for his call-up came. However, when this happened the Todmorden Military Tribunal had ruled out his conscientious objector appeal on the grounds that he had 'attested' to fight and so must join the armed services. In January 1918 Schofield explained all this in a letter to the recruiting officer at Halifax barracks, Captain Moorhouse, requesting him to get Schofield into the R.A.M.C. or into a job as a medical orderly anywhere. The problem was that he had popped a ten shillings note into the envelope as a, "New Year's Gift," to Captain Moorhouse. Sadly for Sam, this was interpreted as a bribe by the military authorities, and Sam was hauled before the magistrates on a charge of attempting to induce Captain Moorhouse to break King's Regulations. Sam could have faced severe punishment, but the magistrates decided to let him off lightly. He was fined £2, or a month in prison, as a warning.

In view of Mr Simpson-Hinchliffe's wholehearted efforts to ensure that no one in the locality escaped the net of conscription without legitimate reason, it may have brought some satisfaction to many to hear, in May 1917, that 'gamekeeper' was about to become 'poacher.' A new order from the War Office stated that no person of military age should occupy the position of Military Representative on Tribunals. At the age of 36, there was no escape for Simpson-Hinchliffe, although he was given a temporary exemption to clear up the affairs of his recently deceased wife. In May 1917 he announced his resignation.

Simpson-Hinchliffe may well have appeared to be the scourge of local Tribunals from time to time, but the tributes paid to him suggest that he had won respect. Mr Joseph Clay, Chairman of the local Rural District Tribunal, suggested that its members should lobby the military authorities to allow Simpson-Hinchliffe to stay on as Military Representative to the end of the war. Clay and his colleagues were well satisfied with his work, describing Simpson-Hinchliffe as, "courteous and willing to listen to anything

Nothing caused more divisions in local society than the workings and decisions of the Military Tribunals.

we had to say." There were more fulsome tributes to him from the Hebden Bridge and Mytholmroyd Tribunals, but the higher military authorities insisted that Simpson-Hinchliffe had to go. He accepted the decision with seeming good humour and enlisted. By March 1918 he had gained a commission in the Motor Transport Section.

Nothing caused more divisions in local society than the workings and decisions of the Military Tribunals. The horrors of modern warfare were known to all by 1916, and it is difficult to blame anyone who wanted to avoid them. If men had to go, however, it was only fair that every plea for exemption was scrutinised carefully. This was the difficult task of those who staffed the Tribunals and who were fully aware that they might be making literally life or death decisions. It was easy, then, to arouse suspicions of malpractice or favouritism. Decisions could be contentious no matter what type of exemption was being discussed, whether on grounds of domestic hardship, ill-health, work of national importance or, most of all, conscience. This last named was a minefield for the Tribunals, who were as likely to face accusations that they were letting men 'get away with it' as accusations that they were being too harsh.

It is no surprise that some Tribunal members felt that the weight of responsibility was too much for them to sustain over a long period. Councillor Edward Sutcliffe, a member of the Hebden Bridge Tribunal from its outset, had never been known for being soft-hearted towards conscientious objectors, but he became disillusioned at the later work imposed on the Tribunals, particularly the innovation that the 'price' of exemption for some men, "whose daily task is one of long and arduous labour," was to join the local Volunteer Training Corps (a First World War version of the later Home Guard). Therefore Councillor Sutcliffe resigned in June 1918, stating that, "The work has become increasingly disagreeable and even repugnant to me."

CHAPTER 13 – KING KHAKI

'King Cotton' once ruled Lancashire's textiles industry, achieving even world dominance. By the outbreak of World War One the crown was slipping in the face of foreign competition. In Todmorden (a Yorkshire town but very much a cotton one) five cotton mills were closed and nine on short time in July 1914. It was widely expected that the industry's dependence on the export trade would mean its death knell in the event of a world war. In contrast, neighbouring Hebden Bridge was relatively prosperous at the outbreak of war. Known sometimes as 'Fustianopolis,' it had gained an international reputation in the manufacture of ready-made fustian garments, and although the industry had peaked, Hebden Bridge still possessed a strong industrial base in terms of the skills and experience of its workforce.

Economic uncertainty at the outbreak of war seemed to confirm the gloomy forecasts of the pessimists as around 500,000 were made redundant nationally in its first few weeks. War does nothing, however, if it does not create jobs, and by September 1914 the first government army contract had gained for Hebden Bridge and district orders for, among other items, two million khaki uniforms. 'King Khaki' was crowned in Hebden Bridge and the army was not the only one of its benefactors, for Redman Bros., at Foster Mill, made most of the duffel coats worn by Royal Navy personnel during the war.

Nevertheless, government contracts did not constitute a constant golden flow of business into the Upper Calder Valley. Clothing manufacturers in other parts of the country were bidding to get their share, and there were often worryingly long intervals between contracts. At the end of April 1915, for example, an editorial in the *Hebden Bridge and District News* commented that the town's staple industry – clothing – was doing so well that its workers had been awarded a war bonus. By September, however, a note of anxiety was being sounded in the local press. Seemingly

> **SAD NEWS AT ASHWORTH & CO.**
> Local mills and workshops were constantly receiving news, good and bad, of their former employees. As the war progressed, the bad news increasingly overshadowed the good. By August 1916 the firm of Thomas Ashworth, shuttlemakers of Hangingroyd Lane, Hebden Bridge, reported that three of its men had been wounded – Privates W. Halstead, Joe Greenwood and Tom Ashworth (son of the head of the firm). Worse still, three had been killed, Privates Francis Sutcliffe, Wilfred Uttley and Wilbert Jackson. By January 1917 another death was added to the list – that of George W. Crabtree of the Royal Scots.

Wilfred Uttley, one of the three former employees of Thomas Ashworth who had been lost by August 1916.
Courtesy of Keith Stansfield

khaki contracts were almost worked out and, for the moment, no more were forthcoming.

In Todmorden too, early fears that the war would bring about total economic collapse proved to be groundless. After a few months of uncertainty, large government orders for cotton goods meant that, "the cotton trade experienced a period of prosperity such had never been known before." (J.A. Lee, *Todmorden and the Great War, 1914-1918*) As early as August 20th two local mills – Hope Street and Ridgefoot – saw their looms working day and night. By the

---
At least four Todmorden firms worked on munitions contracts
---

end of November 1914 many of Todmorden's principal mills were running full time.

The war also created opportunities outside textiles. Ormerod Bros. of Hebden Bridge, became heavily engaged in the making of shells. At least four Todmorden firms worked on munitions contracts, these being Lord Bros. of Canal Street Works, Geo. Whitehead and Sons of Salford Works, A. Kinghorn and Sons of Phoenix Works and Sam Crabtree Ltd. of Kilnhurst Works. With industrial manpower being mopped up by Lord Kitchener's call to arms, plenty of employment opportunities sprung up for women, in munitions and elsewhere. According to J.A. Lee, Todmorden saw women delivering the post and the milk, taking on clerical work and making inroads into the railways as booking clerks, ticket collectors and porters.

'TIRED MUNITION WORKERS': A LITTLE IRONY FROM THE FRONT
Writing in September 1917 of a long spell in the trenches, a Hebden Bridge soldier adds, "We have not had anywhere near so hard a time as before. All the same, I think 'tired munitions workers' have much the best of it, even though a Sunday paper has discovered that we look well, robust, ruddy and hearty, while the workers are pale anaemic and tired looking. It looks as though we are to be envied, but I have no wish to be selfish, and beg to suggest that what does so well for us should be administered to the workers – same hours, same rations, and same pay. It is not fair that we soldiers should have all the advantages, and if it will improve the munition man's lot at all I will willingly start having a few hours off on Saturdays, all day on Sundays, and an occasional holiday."

In spite of the anxieties expressed in September 1915, a retrospective newspaper editorial in December could claim that the Hebden Bridge clothing trade (largely seasonal) had never had such a summer before. The ripples of prosperity had spread from the sewing shops to the weavers, dyeworkers and cutters, whilst local engineering was in good shape. Local mills were extending their premises, with a new weaving shed at Foster Holme for E. Sutcliffe

---
By the end of 1915 the cost of living was increasing at a rate of 27% per annum
---

and Co., a new warehouse at Hangingroyd and expansion at the Nutclough Fustian Manufacturing Society. Wages were rising everywhere.

There was, however, a 'fly in the ointment.' Wages were rising but prices were rising even faster. By the end of 1915 the cost of living was increasing at a rate of 27% per annum, and of greatest concern to the workers was the rise in the price of staples such as bread and milk. As a result there was constant hard bargaining between trades unions and employers over wage rates, and in the autumn of 1916 a pay dispute in the Hebden Bridge clothing industry escalated into a full blown strike which lasted six weeks. Strikes were unusual during the war, but not unknown. The heavy hand of the 1914 Defence of the Realm Act had steered clear of banning strikes, and prominent government figures such as Lloyd George preferred persuasion and appeals to patriotism rather than coercion. The Board of Trade was always anxious to offer its services as an arbitrator, although as the war progressed it could insist on arbitration in the case of a dispute in a key industry. Nevertheless the employers and the trades unions often preferred to lock horns before seeking outside help.

Chapter 13 – King Khaki

Looms weaving at Waterside Mill, Todmorden – c.1913.

Courtesy of Pennine Horizons

In the case of the 1916 local clothing industry dispute, trouble had seemingly been brewing for a long time before things came to a head. The United Garment Workers' Union was demanding pay rises of five shillings per week for male adults, half that amount for juniors and 25% for piece workers, who were mainly female. The sticking point for the employers was this last named group. Of the roughly 2,500 workforce of the Hebden Bridge and district clothing trade, the vast majority was

> By weekend, virtually all the Hebden Bridge clothing factories were at a standstill

female. The employers argued that they were better paid than females at any other clothing centre in the United Kingdom, and that a further pay rise would make it impossible to submit competitive tenders for future government khaki orders. As a result the Masters' Association refused to consider any of the wage demands, either male or female.

The situation was deadlocked and on Tuesday, October 31st 1916, the first workers walked out – at the Nutclough Fustian Manufacturing Company. By weekend, virtually all the Hebden Bridge clothing factories were at a standstill, and some workers in two Todmorden factories had come out in sympathy. The strike was solid, and one or two workers who had remained in their places on Friday were faced by a large group of men and girls, "hooting and shouting," as they left for home. The atmosphere was generally good-humoured, but the girls in particular had showed their persuasive powers earlier that day when a group had marched to Astins', at the top of Tuel Lane, and cajoled the girls there into joining the strike.

> *A strike in wartime was bound to raise passions and the term 'unpatriotic' was frequently bandied about. In 1982 local history researcher, Tom Greenwood, interviewed John Barnes, a stalwart of the local Independent Labour Party, who was twelve at the time of the strike. John remembered groups of strikers going from workshop to workshop bringing out the men and women. He was put in a wheelbarrow by his father and treated as the strikers' mascot. John was a half-timer, spending half a day at work and the other half at school. On his return to school one of his teachers, a local manufacturer's daughter, called him a guttersnipe, but the Head extracted an apology from her.*

That this strike was of some importance nationally was shown by the fact that a question was raised in the House of Commons about the dispute. At a mass meeting at the Co-operative Hall, a resolution was passed by the United Garment Workers' Union indicating its willingness to accept arbitration by the Board of Trade. Nothing happened immediately, but the importance of the local clothing trade to the war effort is indicated by the fact that, under instructions from the War Office, work was re-commenced at one factory, possibly with an increase in pay.

In December 1916, after six weeks, the clothing strike was settled. A meeting of the representatives of the employers and the workers, under the chairmanship of Mr K.C. Doughty K.C., appointed by the Board of Trade, thrashed out an agreement after six hours of deliberations. Compromise was the order of the day. Pay rises were conceded by the employers, although these did not match the initial demands of the garment workers. On top of the pay award, female workers over the age of 18 received a war bonus of one halfpenny an hour. Work was resumed on December 14th 1916 after a dispute which had cost the United Garment Workers' Union over £1000 per week in strike pay.

The pattern of khaki contracts and hard bargaining continued to the end of the war.

In September 1917 it was revealed in the press that the government was yet again about to put in a very large order for fustian pieces. The magnitude of the order was such that, "Local manufacturers will, of course, come in for a share of the work." Not only that, the dyehouses would be kept busy dying the clothing for the army. In its 'Review of the Year 1917,' the *Hebden Bridge and District News* stated that government orders were keeping the looms in the weaving sheds fully occupied, "and will do for some time to come." Day and night working, along with overtime, had been plentiful in 1917, and a large order in April of that year, distributed throughout the Calder Valley, had been given the banner headline of 'A MILLION YARDS OF CLOTH' in the *Leeds Mercury*.

Nevertheless, older textile workers had vivid memories of trade depressions and harder times in their industry in days past. They knew that khaki contracts were not a 'golden goose' that could be totally relied on. Indeed, intermingled with the good news in the press of yet another juicy government order in 1917, there was a more cautionary note suggesting unemployment amongst weavers if the locality had not gained its share. It was a matter of making the best of the good times, so it comes as no surprise to see, in May 1918, another dispute over wages in the clothing trade, accompanied by a strike ballot. This particular

Were these three in Hebden Bridge khaki? Brothers from Colden who all survived the war; from left to right – George, Len and Johnny Collinge.

Courtesy of PennineHorizons

dispute was triggered by nationwide dissatisfaction in the clothing industry at the wage increases announced by the government's Committee of Production late in 1917. The garment workers' representatives argued that these increases compared very unfavourably with those gained by every other trade union. At a union branch meeting held at the Co-operative Hall in Hebden Bridge, the local secretary announced that although strike ballot papers had gone out, the government probably would not allow a strike to proceed because of the number of large government khaki orders going through the factories. This proved to be the case when the Chief Industrial Commissioner, Sir George Askwith, used the government's residual powers to impose arbitration on the dispute.

Whereas 'King Khaki,' along with its associated industries, was flourishing under government contracts, government pressure from another direction was causing production problems. Voluntary enlistment, supplemented by conscription into the army, resulted in a labour shortage just when work was plentiful. In February 1917, the firm of H. Ashworth, shuttle manufacturers of Hebden Bridge, announced that with the death of Private George Wilson Crabtree, it had lost its fourth employee in the war. This was not unusual. In August 1917 the death of Private Vernon Gibson, of High Street, marked the fourth employee of James Hoyle and Sons to be killed, along with one missing. One of the largest manufacturing concerns in the district, the Nutclough Fustian Manufacturing Company, had lost six of its employees by October 1916, but by May 1918 the death of Bertrand Blackburn from dysentery, in Palestine, brought the number to twelve. When Gunners Herbert Sutcliffe and Frank Hartley were killed in March 1917, these were two men who, in the early stages of the war, had each been offered £10 by their employer, R. Thomas

It was a walk-out of workers from Nutclough Mill, Hebden Bridge, which set in motion the clothing strike of 1916.

Courtesy of Pennine Horizons

and Sons, Hebden Bridge, as an inducement to enlist. The transformation in attitude was complete with the introduction of conscription in 1916. The Military Tribunals were now full of local employers desperate to keep their men by arguing that they were playing a vital part in the completion of war contracts.

> *If the war brought 'boom' times to textile and engineering concerns, not all trades prospered. A reflective piece in the Hebden Bridge Times of February 11th 1916, entitled, 'WAR AND UNCERTAIN FARES,' constituted a lament for the 'cabby' and the local carrying business. Several old established businesses had been forced to put up the shutters. Individual cabmen (the horse-drawn taxis of their day) were also going out of business and Mr Walter Greenwood, a long serving 'cabby' based at Hebden Bridge station, was one of these. His explanation was simple – that 'fares' had got few and far-between. The very old posting and carrying firm of Sunderlands, of King Street, had closed down the previous week, and on Tuesday an auction had been held of all its assets, "including horses, wagons, cabs, waggonettes, gears and other horse-keeping paraphernalia." A large attendance of horse-dealers and carriers from all over the country had converged on the event. In recognising the end of an era, the whole tone of the piece was one of regret at the passing of such a familiar element of local life, the drivers (and even the horses) being known to all the community. And the causes for all this? The high prices of horses and feeding stuffs, along with the scarcity of labour.*

The labour shortage situation was no better in Todmorden. In May 1916 a meeting was held in the Town Hall by the Women's War Employment Committee to look for solutions to the problem of the shortage of labour. Todmorden's cotton factories had always been heavily reliant on women, but it was suggested at the meeting that many women formerly employed in this way were now living off the war allowances paid out to soldiers' families. Also munitions offered a better paid prospect for those who wanted to work. Various schemes

hundreds of looms and other machines were standing idle due to the labour shortage

were put forward, but were considered to be impracticable, including importing women from other parts of the country and importing boys from the Isle of Man on three year contracts. In the end it was decided to survey the needs of the Todmorden employers. Those who undertook this task reported back to the Committee in June 1916. The findings were that hundreds of looms and other machines were standing idle due to the labour shortage and it was estimated that around 700 women and girls with previous experience in textiles were at home. It was decided to send letters appealing to them to resume employment as far as their domestic duties allowed, and in this respect part-time work was a possibility. Little more was heard of this scheme and it seems likely that the outcomes were disappointing.

CHAPTER 14 – FEELING THE STRAIN

In fighting a war on a previously unimaginable scale, a war in which large swathes of society were directly involved, both at home and on the fighting fronts, the government needed to promote the idea of unity. The British people needed to feel that sacrifices were being borne equally between all classes and individuals. Otherwise the rot from within would undermine and possibly destroy the war effort. Along with conscription (and exemptions from it) and industrial relations, the most persistent issue that threatened to fracture the unity of the nation was that of the price and availability of the necessities of life.

At the outset of war, a letter to the *Hebden Bridge Times* had little time for discussing the 'pros' and 'cons' of British involvement, but expressed anxiety about the price of milk. A

German 'U'-boats increasingly sank merchant ships as they approached British shores.

---

meeting of the Todmorden and District Trades and Labour Council, held in 1915, saw speakers railing against the rapid rise of milk and wheat prices. Anger was expressed about the greed of monopolists and a resolution was passed demanding that the government take control of both food supply and prices. Two-thirds of Britain's food supply came from overseas, including 80% of its wheat and most of its sugar. People understood that war was bound to disrupt this flow, a trend that could only worsen as German 'U'-boats increasingly sank merchant ships as they approached British shores. Scarcity in a free market could only mean rising prices, but the government was slow to respond to the repeated pleas of trades union and Labour Party leaders for it to take control of food supply and prices. It could argue, truthfully, that wages were rising but only in areas such as munitions work could wages keep pace with rising prices.

If self-help was to be the answer, then the watchword was 'economy.' This was the message hammered out by central government, local councils and even from the pulpit, with housewives being the main target. In April 1916, for example, the West Riding County Council sponsored a demonstration of economy cooking by a Miss Irons at the Co-operative Hall, Todmorden. It was very well attended. Such pinpricks did not recommend themselves to the local Labour Party and Trades Council, which held a 'Protest Meeting' over food prices at the Todmorden Town Hall in November 1916. The familiar demand was made for government control of food supply and prices. If this sounded radical, then Mr Joseph Hyder, the Secretary of the Land Nationalisation Society, based in London, had gone one step further by advocating in the press the take-over of all agricultural land by the government in order to prevent, "the manipulation of the market by unscrupulous speculators."

The government moved slowly but move it did. By the end of 1916 the Board of Trade had put controls on the price of milk, but 1917 proved to be the crucial year. From February of that year, Germany attempted to deliver a knockout blow to Britain by adopting the strategy of unrestricted submarine warfare. Whereas the targets before had been the shipping of Britain and her allies, now neutral ships would be attacked also, the aim being to

---

In the spring of 1917, potatoes were not to be had at all for two or three weeks in Todmorden.

---

starve Britain into surrender in six months. The results were drastic. In April 1917, enemy action sank 169 British ships and 204 allied or neutral vessels, representing a loss of almost one million tons, or one-quarter of Britain's imports. In that month alone 46,000 tons of meat were lost at sea, along with 85,000 tons of sugar from February to June. Stocks of wheat and flour were down to two months. By mid-1917, bread and potatoes had doubled in price from 1915, with similar increases in the costs of sugar, butter, milk, cheese, bacon and the cheaper cuts of meat. Drastic price rises went hand-in-hand with scarcity. In the spring of 1917, potatoes were not to be had at all for two or three weeks in Todmorden. Swedes and other substitutes were resorted to. There is no doubt that 1917 saw the nation really beginning to feel the strain.

> **WAS NOWHERE SAFE?**
> *Whilst it was understandable that stretcher bearers might easily fall prey to the indiscriminate fire of machine guns and artillery on the battlefield, the sinking of hospital ships seems to be more a matter of cold calculation. This was the case when the clearly marked British hospital ship, Britannic, was sunk by a 'U'- boat in November 1916. A local member of the Royal Army Medical Corps, named Woodhead, was reported as missing, presumed dead.*

Still reluctant to impose rationing, the government Food Controller, Lord Devonport, embarked upon a huge newspaper and poster campaign in February 1917. 'Eat Less Bread,' was the message on the posters, the aim being to shift consumption away from grain (mostly imported) to meat (more likely to be home produced). Working class families, however, were highly reliant on bread, which was relatively cheap and filling. Meat was largely a luxury. It was virtually impossible to persuade the working classes to eat less bread. Therefore one answer was to tamper with the bread. From March 1917, by government order to bakeries, such items as maize and barley were mixed in with the wheat. Hence the arrival of 'Khaki bread,' dark of colour and strange of taste (but seemingly more nutritious) which Todmorden people were forewarned about as early as December 1916. No doubt there was plenty of grumbling about this, but no resorting to extreme measures in the Upper Calder Valley. Elsewhere, in the poorest urban areas, there were reports of free soup kitchens and even sporadic food riots in Liverpool and London.

A not very successful appeal as bread was the working class staple.
Courtesy of Bankfield Museum

One advantage enjoyed by this area was its mix of the urban and the rural. Early in 1917 local councils set up Land Cultivation Sub-Committees, the result being a circular to all local farmers asking what area of land each could put under the plough for the growing of such crops as oats, swedes and potatoes. Also

The 'U'- boat was to be countered by the spade.

they were asked whether they were prepared to let out any land for allotments. This was part of a great movement to counteract the diminishing food supply from abroad by making Britain as

Chapter 14 – Feeling The Strain

self-sufficient as possible. The 'U'- boat was to be countered by the spade. From December 1916 local authorities had been given the power to take over unoccupied land, with or without the owner's consent, and turn it over to growing food. Common land, parks and playing fields were also dug up and planted.

Local councils did their best to take the lead, but availability of unused tillable land was a problem. In February 1917 Wadsworth Parish Council bought Carr Head Farm and then leased it to Mr John Greenwood on condition that he sub-let the land for allotments. It was suggested that poultry keeping would be the best option. The ubiquitous Mr Simpson-Hinchliffe was quickly to the fore, and he offered free use of a piece of land at Bank Top, Cragg Vale, on which his factory workers could grow vegetables. Local council meetings at Heptonstall and Mytholmroyd did not at first seem to arouse much enthusiasm, but six allotments were taken up at Heptonstall Slack in March 1917, and requests for vegetable plots at Mytholmroyd grew from two to twenty in the course of a week. Here plots were leased out at a farthing a yard for the duration of the war. Finding spare land was still a difficulty, but the fashion for digging was spreading up the valley to Charlestown, Thistlebottom and Mankinholes.

Lend these Men to the State
while the ploughing season lasts.

Ploughing is a skilled occupation. Ploughmen cannot be improvised. There is no time to teach men brought from other occupations. The ploughing season is already here. Without the work which your men can do, the land cannot be used to the best advantage. So urgent is the matter that you are asked to call your employees together, within the next 24 hours if possible, and to find out who among them can plough. In many cases their Registration Cards will show this.

You are asked to send the names and ages of these men to the Director of the Agricultural Section, National Service Department, St. Ermin's, London, S.W., together with an offer to release them for temporary work on the land until the end of the sowing season.

ENROL TO-DAY
For National Service
and back up the men in the trenches.

Producing more food 'at home' was becoming a government priority.

It is hardly surprising that the local allotment movement got off to a slightly uneasy start. Most mill workers would have had little or no experience of horticulture. The working day was a long and hard one, and the working week was at least five and a half, sometimes six days. Perhaps some felt that they had little energy or inclination for digging during their short weekends.

> *In some instances, working on the Sabbath proved to be an issue. Whereas the Archbishop of Canterbury issued a pastoral letter sanctioning Sunday work for Anglicans, the half-yearly meeting of the Hebden Bridge and District Baptist Churches, held in May 1917, declared that Sunday work on allotments was against God's law, prospective famine or not.*

Nevertheless, although the taking up of allotments may have had a slow start, both at national and local levels, it soon picked up momentum. The government's Food Production Department offered advice to new horticulturists, and the prospect of growing one's own food at a time of shortage soon began to appeal to more and more. The number of allotments doubled in 1917, and by the end of the war it had reached four times its 1914 level. This represented over 90,000 acres of extra land under cultivation.

Worthwhile as this appeal to self-help was, in the eyes of the trades unions and Labour Party it was merely a sticking plaster solution to really severe problems. In May 1917, local trades union delegates attended a Food Conference at Wakefield organised by the Federated Trades Councils of Yorkshire. A resolution was passed urging the government to purchase all essential foodstuffs, commandeer ships and transport, and put food on the market at controlled prices, "to secure the prevention of famine for the people of this country."

Similar sentiments were expressed at meetings at Todmorden and Sowerby Bridge. At the latter gathering, the Sowerby Division Labour Party added an extra recommendation – that 'food vigilance committees' should be appointed locally to ensure that any food distribution organised by municipal authorities should be done fairly. Such committees had come into being in both Hebden Bridge and Todmorden by June 1917.

Up to this point the government had relied on cajoling and appeals for economy and avoidance of waste. Clearly, however, there was a rising mood of discontent in the country over the food issue and the government needed, above all, to promote the feeling that sacrifices were being shared by all. At last, in June 1917, the government took a step in taking its responsibilities more seriously. The new Food

> *In June 1917 the Hebden Bridge District Council created a War Committee, and it called a public meeting to consider various food orders made by both the government and the local Food Controller. It took a full hour for the clerk to the Council, Mr Sam Ogden, to read out regulations relating to such items as milk, bread and sugar. Eating out also came under scrutiny. By the Public Meals Act – applying to restaurants, hotels and boarding houses – no meat could be served on 'meatless days;' no potatoes except on 'meatless days;' amounts strictly limited, e.g. no more than two ounces of bread at breakfast.*

---
profits from agriculture had increased fivefold between 1914 and 1917

Controller, Lord Rhondda, brought food supply under the effective control of the state. Those who complained of profiteering had not been far short of the mark as far as agriculture was concerned. Big landowners and food distributors had done well out of scarcity and high prices, for profits from agriculture had increased fivefold between 1914 and 1917. The War Agricultural Executive Committee was now set up to bring more efficiency into this sector. Farmers had to concentrate on essential foods such as wheat, barley and potatoes. Farmers disobeying instructions would be contravening the Defence of the Realm Act. The Women's Land Army was created to deal with the labour shortage on the land.

Reorganising the food supply was all well and good, but it did not solve scarcity overnight. Fair distribution could only be achieved by rationing. Under the general guidance of the government, this was organised at a local level under the control of local Food Controllers.

The first fully fledged system of rationing came in August 1917 when Lord Rhondda ordered local authorities to appoint Food Committees to administer a new scheme of sugar distribution. The local Food Controller was to set the price and the public were to apply for sugar cards. They needed them to register with a retailer and would be allowed a certain amount weekly, which would vary along with the local stocks. Sugar seemed to be the 'guinea pig' in the rationing experiment. It was a *want* rather than a *need*, but most people regarded it as so essential that it effectively became a need. Sugar cards had to be applied for at post offices by the end of September 1917, and complaints soon arose about the petty bureaucracy involved. An applicant had to be absolutely precise in his or her description of employment. 'Railway employee,' was not precise enough. Finer distinctions had to be made, for example 'booking office clerk' or 'railway porter.' People complained not only about the irrelevance of such 'nit picking,' but also about the hefty fines which could be imposed - £100 or six months in prison – for supposed misrepresentation.

Sugar seemed to be emblematic of scarcity as a whole. Milk could be well provided locally (price was the sticking point here); bread was plentiful with the introduction of the despised 'Khaki bread'; but sugar, now that was another matter. On June 29th 1917, the following notice was to be found in the local press:- 'Mrs H. Gudger, proprietor of Edge End Farm, close to Callis Wood, which provides teas to small parties, advises visitors that, due to the sugar shortage, visitors should bring their own.' Later, in August, amongst the weighty items on the agenda at the annual meeting of the Yorkshire Federation of Trades Councils, held at the Weavers' Institute in Todmorden, were

> *it was local common knowledge that one Todmorden man had four hundredweight of sugar stored in his cellar!*

the 'Russian Revolution' and 'Food Profiteering.' With regard to the former, a vigorous debate ensued with at least one delegate advocating that the British working classes should follow the Russian example. With regard to the latter, the temperature in the room was raised even further when Mr T.A. Taylor stated that it was local common knowledge that one Todmorden man had four hundredweight of sugar stored in his cellar! Food hoarding was now a criminal offence, and in October 1917 a Mytholmroyd man, Mr Charles Barker, was fined £15 for being caught with one hundredweight of sugar in his house.

Rationing of a sort had arrived, but it was exercised very much at a local rather than a governmental level. As at Hebden Bridge, Todmorden had its Food Controller and its Food Control Committee. In September 1917 other goods followed sugar onto the Todmorden Food Controller's list for which maximum prices were set, such as meat, margarine, butter and tea. There were general shortages of other consumer goods, whether on the rationed list or not – lard, cheese, currants, apples. Beer supplies suffered also and some public houses in Todmorden closed entirely for weeks on end, the doleful sign of 'No Beer' hanging in their windows.

> *The heavy hand of the Food Controller at Hebden Bridge fell on William Greaves, confectioner of Bridge Gate, in September 1917. He was summoned to court for breaching the Cake and Pastry Order in that he had, "added an edible substance to the exterior of four coconut buns." This substance was sprinkled coconut, which breached the object of the Order which was to prevent pastry being made more attractive. Grim days indeed!*
>
> *This was the first case of its kind and so Greaves was only given a light fine, five shillings, as a warning to others. Nevertheless, only a few months later Albert Probert, confectioner of St. George's Square, faced a similar summons for making four scones that contained 5% of sugar, when they should have had none. This was proved by food analysis, and the magistrates showed that they meant business this time by fining Probert £2.*

A strange paradox was now coming into play. By the autumn of 1917, the system of merchant ships sailing in convoy, protected by destroyers, had much diminished the 'U'- boat menace. Supplies from abroad were improving, augmented by more self-sufficiency at home. A good potato harvest in 1917 had halved their price. Wheat yields were improving due to the shift from dairy to arable farming and the wheat harvest of 1917 was the best of the century. Nevertheless shortages persisted because of poor distribution. Rationing operated at a local level and related to maximum prices rather than quantities that could be purchased. There was some suspicion among the working classes that Food Control Committees were dominated by traders and businessmen who saw to it that shops in better class areas were well stocked whilst the poor had to queue for limited stocks elsewhere. The system was entirely in the hands of local retailers. Other than issuing a string of Food Orders, the government's only interference was to subsidise the price of bread in order to keep it reasonably cheap. Hence the rise of local Food Vigilance Committees to challenge what they saw as any wrongdoing.

> *Suspicions of wrongdoing were sometimes justified and a reporter in the Labour supporting Daily Herald added fuel to the flames when he produced an article entitled 'HOW THEY STARVE AT THE RITZ.' Having visited the restaurant 'undercover', his article exposed the huge self-indulgence of the rich. Apparently any luxury food or drink could be purchased, in any quantity, with complete disregard for the official restrictions on restaurants. The article was mass produced as a leaflet and distributed nationally to thousands of factories.*

The article did not fill the streets with thousands of protesters. What was already filling the streets from the autumn of 1917 was the urge to queue. Uncertainty of supplies meant that housewives across the country were congregating outside any shop which was suspected of having any. In big cities queues could become thousands strong, and in December 1917 a queue of over 3,000 was reported outside a London shop which had stocks of margarine.

December was also the peak month locally. In Todmorden a rumour of incoming stocks could result in a shop being besieged. Queuing was usually done in an orderly fashion, but sometimes order was only maintained by the presence of police and special constables. The climax in Todmorden came on Friday and Saturday, December 21st and 22nd, with a queue of between four and five hundred outside one shop. It took at least three hours to be served. Hebden Bridge found itself in similar circumstances, and a letter of complaint to the local Food Committee stressed that the problem was being aggravated by people from outside the area coming in early by tram or train and grabbing the first places in the queues. Again, self-help seems to have been the answer as the Todmorden Food Committee met with local food retailers and agreed to a local system of rationing with regard to butter, margarine and tea. Ration cards were issued to local families. At Hebden Bridge and elsewhere locally, similar schemes were being introduced.

> *The climax in Todmorden came on Friday and Saturday, December 21st and 22nd, with a queue of between four and five hundred outside one shop.*

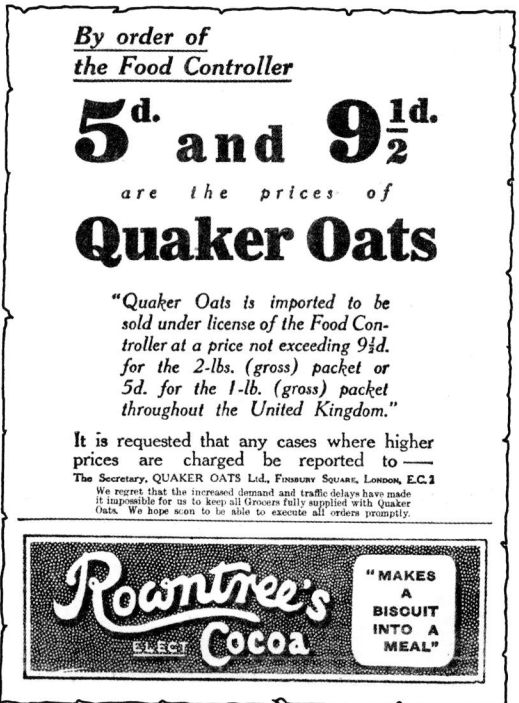

The Food Controller even gets a mention in this advertisement.

The government was left in no doubt that shortages and queuing were creating a serious situation. The source of its information was rock solid – the censors. Letters home from soldiers were vetted, and those who had recently been on leave were of particular interest. The frequent mention of food shortages and queues convinced the Head Censor, based at Calais, that this was having a bad effect on soldiers' morale. The feeling that the sacrifices of war were not being shared equally could, in the opinion of the Head Censor, undermine the war effort. At the same time, January 1918, the Hebden Bridge Food Vigilance Committee was expressing the very same sentiments. This Committee, comprising representatives of trades unions, Co-operative Societies and the Independent Labour Party, called a meeting to discuss 'The Food Question,' at the Co-operative Hall. Speaking to a packed room, containing many women, Mr Greenwood Pickles, the Chairman, condemned the food queues and demanded that the *government* should ensure that all got their fair share, rich or poor. A scheme such as the Sugar Cards was demanded.

It took a long time for the government to get the message – that rationing was the answer.

Courtesy of Bankfield Museum

THE OTHER SIDE OF THE COIN

In February 1918 a soldier writing home expressed surprise at people in Hebden Bridge and district, "grumbling and grousing about being a bit short of food." He urged them to think about his life, facing constant danger in a wet and muddy trench, surviving on hard biscuits and bully beef.

It is probable that government representatives were more influenced by the arguments of the Head Censor than by those of Mr Greenwood Pickles, but nevertheless the end result was the desired one. The Ministry of Food instituted general food rationing in February 1918, beginning with meat and extending to butter, margarine and lard by July 1918. A household registered with a grocer and a butcher and was issued with ration coupons. The weekly allowance per person was 15 ounces of meat, 5 ounces of bacon (about four rashers), 8 ounces of sugar and 4 ounces of butter/margarine. Even so, local Food Committees still controlled the rationing of tea, cheese and jam. Maximum prices for goods were still prescribed. These simple regulations solved the queuing problem almost overnight. People may have felt that their rations were miserly but at least, notwithstanding the inevitable 'black market' that sprang up, the system was felt to be fair.

That is not to say that there were no more problems locally with regard to food. Considering that at the very outbreak of war, letters to the press were expressing anxiety about the price of milk, it was ironic that disputes over this issue rumbled on throughout 1918. A Milk Dealers' Association had been set up by local farmers in 1917, and it had already clashed with the newly appointed Hebden Bridge and District Food Controller in late 1917 by putting up the price of milk from five pence to sixpence a quart without his permission. There was much public resentment at this and the Food Controller allowed this price to stand for one week only before it returned to its former price. The Dealers were unhappy but accepted it.

Another issue arose in 1918, this time over the making of butter. The Food Committees from Todmorden to Sowerby Bridge sent a

---

The farmers were undoubtedly a feisty lot

---

stern notice to all local farmers that all the milk produced should be made available to the public, and none should be set aside for the making of butter. Farmers had been pursuing a profitable little side line in this respect, but the Controllers insisted that butter was a luxury and the practice must stop. The farmers were undoubtedly a feisty lot, and were at loggerheads with the local Food Committees again in May 1918 over the price of milk set for June and July. A brief delivery strike on the part of the farmers ensued which began on a Sunday. In his book on the war years in Todmorden, J.A. Lee painted an engaging picture of householders in their Sunday clothes, and carrying all manner of receptacles, visiting farms and buying milk. The strike was soon over, but the price of milk loomed large in the public's consciousness and price controls were still in operation in early 1919.

CHAPTER 15 – KEEP RIGHT ON

The year 1916, "has passed away unwept, unhonoured and unsung by Hebden Bridge residents." This was the opening line of the editorial of the *District News* of January 5th 1917. The editor then went on to comment that conscription had brought the war home to people in a way the previous two years had quite failed to do. The deaths of 52 Hebden Bridge and Mytholmroyd men were recorded for 1916. As the war ground on into 1917, with no end in sight, and yet onwards into 1918, the contemporary song by Harry Lauder, *Keep Right on to the End of the Road,* could not have been more appropriate.

Coal shortages became a real problem in the cold winter months of 1917.
Courtesy of Pennine Horizons

'Though the way be long,
let your hearts be strong…

Though you're tired and you're weary,
just journey on.'

Such sentiments struck a chord as the privations of war increasingly imposed themselves on people's lives, and for those who had menfolk serving abroad, the mounting casualty lists added a persistent strain of anxiety to everyday life. The hardships on the Home Front did not end at food shortages. Perhaps second only to food, the increasing scarcity of coal had most impact on people's everyday lives. As early as October 1915 the Board of Trade declared that there was a problem due to the number of colliers who were enlisting. The vast majority of people's homes were heated by coal, and demand for it was increasing as industry geared up for war. The result was a rapid increase in price, and in 1915 a sub-committee of the Todmorden Town Council was negotiating with local suppliers over the question of prices. Coal was also used to produce gas and electricity for lighting, and the Todmorden Town Council found that it could save around £400 per annum by restricting street lighting.

As with food, the government was reluctant to interfere other than to ban Guy Fawkes bonfires from 1916 and preach the need for 'economy.' Again as with food, 1917 was a turning point. It was a very cold year, especially the first few months, and in the cities the police were having to control crowds seeking coal at railway distribution centres. In October, coal rationing was introduced in London. Local authorities could do little about supply, but the Retail Coal Prices Order (1917) allowed them to deal with price, and in November 1917 the Mytholmroyd Urban District Council published a schedule of local coal prices. Coal Committees and Coal Controllers sprung up in all areas. Fuel Overseers had even wider powers. In January 1918 Mr J.A. Head, the Borough Engineer, was appointed to this position which gave him control over Todmorden's coal, gas and electricity prices. Nevertheless supply was a constant problem, and not just for coal itself. As a by-product of gas production, coke was a cheap alternative to coal and was especially favoured for heating factories and public buildings. On January 15th 1918, the log book of Hebden Bridge National School (now Hebden Royd Primary School) records that the Chairman of the Governors, the Vicar, sent the Infants home after one hour because the absence of coke meant that there was no heating. The children were told to stay away the following day also. If they could not stand the intense cold, neither could some of the adults. A large factory in Hebden Bridge had to close for the day on January 15th for the same reason – no coke.

At least the children of Hebden Bridge National School, enjoyed the cold weather.

> **UNPATRIOTIC JOY- RIDING**
> *An unusual aspect of the fuel shortage came to light in March 1918. At Garstang Petty Sessions a Blackpool man was fined £1 for, "improper use of petrol." The culprit was caught joy-riding and his passengers were each fined 10 shillings. One of these was a William Sutcliffe from Hebden Bridge.*

As if coal shortages were not enough, attempts to deal with the problem had an unintended consequence. Local restrictions on street lighting from 1915 were publicised as a precautionary measure against zeppelin attack, but councils were happy enough to save money on their gas or electricity bills. The unintended consequence, however, was a spate of accidents in the darkened streets. In October 1916, as a result of two nurses falling into the canal and drowning, the Hebden Bridge Council ordered that all dangerous street corner kerbs should be whitened and a white band put around tramway standards. Whilst agreeing with the measures, Alderman Crossley complained that street lighting restrictions were absurd in that railway

> *Mrs Alice Bateman of Oxford Street, Hebden Bridge, was drowned in the canal near Stubbing Holme*

stations (always fully lit and a law unto themselves) received information about prospective zeppelin attacks fully three hours in advance – ample time in which to extinguish street lights.

Perhaps it was a pity that Alderman Crossley's ideas were not more fully investigated, for in November 1916 Mrs Alice Bateman of Oxford Street, Hebden Bridge, was drowned in the canal near Stubbing Holme, although her friend was rescued. It may have been in response to these fatalities that the police allowed twenty additional lamps to be lit in and around Hebden Bridge in December 1916. Nevertheless the masking of street lamps lasted until the war ended in 1918. Lighting restrictions were not confined to the streets. Private properties had to be suitably 'blacked out' in the face of the perceived zeppelin threat, and the courts were kept busy with breaches of this regulation. Thomas McEnery, for example, Catholic priest at the Presbytery, Hebden Bridge, was fined £1 in March 1916 under the Defence of the Realm Act for not obscuring a light in his house after nightfall. Perhaps the gradual onset of darker nights caught people unawares in October 1916, for there was a spate of cases in that month, including those of Fred Jagger, tripe dresser of Weasel Hall, and James Mitchell, tailor of Market Street, Hebden Bridge. However, these two, and the other miscreants of that month, were each fined only 10 shillings as opposed to the £1 which poor Father McEnery had been forced to fork out in March.

In the face of casualties, shortages and restrictions, how much anti-war sentiment was felt in the Upper Calder Valley? In August 1916 the government took a gamble in producing and releasing a propaganda film entitled *The Battle of the Somme*. It painted a realistic but not over graphic picture of trench warfare and

Chapter 15 – Keep Right On

the 'over the top' sequence was staged. It was shown at the Hippodrome, Todmorden, between October 19th and 21st, and was advertised as, "the film all the world is going to see." In fact, around twenty million people in Britain saw the film over a six week period. It might have caused horror and revulsion. Seemingly it did not. Sympathy was felt for the fighting men, but this was intermingled with a strong sense of pride and an increased commitment to not only fighting the war, but winning it.

The year 1917, however, was a terrible year in terms of the fighting, epitomised by the Battle of Passchendaele (near Ypres), a British attack which began in July and ground to a halt

> *52 local soldiers had been killed in 1916, three times that number had been lost in 1917.*

in a quagmire three months later, with huge loss of life on both sides. The editor of the *Hebden Bridge and District News*, in his 'Review of the Year' in December 1917, introduced it with the words, "Sorrow has overshadowed pleasure." Whilst noting that government orders were keeping the weaving sheds busy, he also lamented that whilst 52 local soldiers had been killed in 1916, three times that number had been lost in 1917. The total number of Hebden Bridge lads who had been lost in the war now numbered over 200. The editor seems to have been referring to Hebden Bridge alone rather than the district around it. How firm did commitment to the war stay in the face of such losses? Judging by the evidence of two events in the Calder Valley it remained very firm.

In June 1917 a branch of the National Association of Discharged Sailors and Soldiers was formed at the Weavers' Institute in Todmorden. Its aim was to act as a pressure group to provide better state pensions for discharged servicemen and their dependents, along with better allowances for the care of disabled servicemen. There was also dissatisfaction at government 'red tape' causing delays in payments. However, a group of dissatisfied ex-servicemen could be a volatile element in society, exerting pressure in whatever

> *This was like a red rag to a bull to the ex-servicemen,*

direction it chose, as was proved later in the year. In November 1917, at the invitation of the Independent Labour Party, Mrs Philip Snowden was due to speak at a

---

PALS TO THE END

A cohort of 55 Hebden Bridge men joined the army together in May 1915. Many were drafted into the Royal Fusiliers, 'Public Schools' Battalion, and found themselves engaged in the bitter fighting on the Somme in 1916. Two of them, Edwin Jagger of Windsor Road and Harry Sutcliffe of Queen's Terrace, were very close friends. Therefore, in August 1916, when Private Sutcliffe ventured out of the trenches to help a wounded officer, and was shot in the head, Lance Corporal Jagger did not hesitate to go over the top to help both. Sutcliffe had been killed instantly and Jagger himself was shot dead.

Harry Sutcliffe of Queen's Terrace; killed with his pal, Edwin Jagger.

public meeting in Todmorden Town Hall. Mrs Snowden, a renowned 'left-winger,' had founded the Women's Peace Crusade calling for a negotiated peace. This was like a red rag to a bull to the ex-servicemen, who immediately suspected that pacifism was afoot. Having sent a strong letter of protest to the Town Council for allowing the Town Hall to be used for such a purpose, the protesters took matters into their own hands. On the evening of the meeting they blocked the entrances to the Town Hall. A large crowd assembled, largely in favour of the ex-servicemen, and the police stayed passive. As a result the meeting had to be abandoned.

> **A GRATEFUL NATION?**
> In the House of Commons, in June 1916, the Labour Member for Attercliffe (Sheffield) asked the Pensions Minister to look into the case of Private Smith, an ex-serviceman of Mytholmroyd. He had lost his right arm during the war and was receiving a government pension. On learning that Smith was left-handed, the Pensions Department had written to Smith to inform him that his pension would be reduced by two shillings and nine pence per week. The Secretary to the Pensions Minister said that he would look into the matter.

The following day (a Sunday) Mrs Snowden was due to appear at the Co-operative Hall in Hebden Bridge. The outcome was more or less the same. The Hebden Bridge branch of the Association of Discharged Sailors and Soldiers had only been formed in November, but it now found immediate employment. Around fifty men marched on the Co-operative Hall, but rather than blocking the meeting they hi-jacked it by taking over the platform. Whatever Mrs Snowden was going to say will never be known, for the ex-servicemen were determined to stop her. Their President, Mr J. Greenwood, declared from the platform that the I.L.P. (Independent Labour Party) and Mrs Snowden, "have come here to preach peace at any price." He also alleged that one I.L.P. member had referred to a family which had five or six men in the armed forces as, "a family of fools."

At this point things became heated because a proportion of those present disagreed with the pronouncements of Mr Greenwood, and arguments broke out all over the room. Fuel was added to the flames when Mr Harry Shepherd rose to speak. He was a member of a renowned fighting family of Fern Villas, Hebden Bridge, and he had lost a leg at the Dardanelles in 1915. His impassioned anti-pacifist speech caused such uproar that when the Chairman of the local I.L.P., Mr J. W. Crowther, attempted to respond from the platform, his words were drowned by renditions of patriotic songs from the ex-soldiers. Further disturbance was caused by the arrival at this point of a contingent of the Todmorden branch of the Association of Discharged Sailors and Soldiers. It was clear that the meeting was beyond recall and Mrs Snowden, who had been quietly waiting in the wings to speak, slipped away via a side exit.

> **EXCEPTIONAL FAMILIES – THE SHEPHERDS**
> The Shepherd family of Fern Villas, Nazebottom, Hebden Bridge, made a notable contribution to the war effort. The head of the household, Harry Shepherd, was wounded at Gallipoli in July 1915, and was later fitted with an artificial leg. Three sons – James, Arthur and Levi – also served. James was wounded and Levi sailed with an Arctic convoy to Russia in 1918. Here he became embroiled on the side of the 'White' Russians in the civil war against the Bolsheviks. This extended family also included Tom and Walton Hodgson. Tom was wounded at Gallipoli whilst Walton, a regular soldier, fought his way through all the early battles on the Western Front, was wounded, but suffered more wounds in April 1916, in Mesopotamia, from which he died.

The abandonment of these two meetings at Todmorden and Hebden Bridge tells us something about the mood of one section of

Chapter 15 – Keep Right On

local society with reference to the pursuance of the war, but it does not give the full picture. The Association of Discharged Sailors and Soldiers had the prime aims of providing more financial help for ex-servicemen and their dependents, and helping the more able to find employment. However, they could also be an intimidating force in not only opposing what they took to be pacifism, but also in not allowing unwelcome views to be heard.

> The letters to the press after the Co-operative Hall debacle mainly supported the protesters, but a letter from the secretary of the local I.L.P., Mr J. Wheelhouse of Eton Street, Hebden Bridge, pointed out the irony of ex-servicemen preventing, "freedom of expression," for which principle Britain was helping smaller nations in the fight against an autocratic Germany.

At a meeting of the Sowerby I.L.P. Federation, held at the Trades Club in Hebden Bridge, in May 1918, Mr J.W. Crowther laid out the aim of the I.L.P. as being, "to bring about an early cessation of hostilities on a just and permanent basis." This would seem to have been a reasonable enough statement but at this point wholly impracticable. The Germans had launched a massive attack in March which had carried them across the old battlefields of the Somme to within forty miles of Paris. Mr Crowther admitted the problem by saying that the I.L.P. was, "compelled by force of circumstances on the Western Front to remain silent in regard to peace propaganda."

Mr Crowther was an old anti-war warrior, having been prominent in organising the 'No Conscription' meeting in 1916 and the one due to have been addressed by Mrs Snowden, in November 1917, both of which had ended in

hooting, shouting and throwing a rotten egg.

chaos. Therefore, with Germany still in possession of conquered land, he must have known that any talk of a just peace at this point was going to be equated with out-an-out pacifism, and therefore very unpopular. This was demonstrated by the continued failure of the local I.L.P. to acquire a public hall for the wider dissemination of its views. In June 1918 the I.L.P. mustered at the fairground in Hebden Bridge to hear Mr Harker, of Burnley, speaking on 'Socialism and a Conclusive Peace.' The venue in July was some vacant ground opposite the Dusty Miller in Mytholmroyd, where some young lads delayed the start of the meeting by hooting, shouting and throwing a rotten egg. Later assemblies that summer took place in and around St George's Square, Hebden Bridge, and seem to have gone off peacefully enough.

The views of the I.L.P., then, seem to have been greeted with suspicion at best and with anger at worst by local people. To be constantly advocating peace whilst Germany still posed a threat seemed to many to be simply pacifism and a betrayal of those who had lost their lives in fighting German militarism. On the other hand there must have been some who thought that the war had gone on long enough, but kept silent in the face of intimidating forces around them.

CHAPTER 16 – MONEY, MONEY, MONEY

Wars cost money. A war fought on a worldwide scale for over four years was financially crippling to Britain, with an army and a navy to support, trade and industry dislocated, supplies destroyed by 'U' – boat attacks and subsidies being paid out to allies. A government spokesman in Hebden Bridge stated that by 1916 the war was costing the government the staggering sum of £5 million *per day*. Increased taxation could only have covered a small fraction of such huge costs whilst incurring unpopularity in a nation which the government needed to keep 'onside.' Selling overseas assets and borrowing money from abroad went some way to keeping Britain financially afloat, but the main thrust of the government's efforts went towards borrowing money from its own people.

Saving money and helping the war effort at the same time.
Courtesy of Bankfield Museum

In July 1916 a War Savings Week was announced in Hebden Bridge. All citizens were urged to buy government War Savings Certificates at fifteen shillings and sixpence each, with a tax free return. This was followed up in September 1916 when, following a public meeting at the Victoria Hall, a War Savings Association was set up, linking up with the National Committee in London. Not to be outdone, the rural parishes set up their own War Savings Committees, and at a meeting at Crimsworth Council School, in November 1916, Wadsworth adopted its own scheme. Miss Shaw of Halifax, the local representative of the National Committee, gave a very good outline of what this entailed. First of all she stressed the patriotic aspect of the scheme, lending money for the government's war efforts, and in so doing helping the soldiers in their heroic struggle. Secondly she promoted the financial advantages, telling the well-attended meeting that a fifteen shillings and sixpence certificate would accrue interest and be worth £5 (tax free) after five years.

The price of a certificate, however, would have made substantial inroads into the wages of an average worker. Miss Shaw had the answer. If Wadsworth formed its own War Savings Committee, each of its members would pay a small weekly subscription. Once the total had reached fifteen shillings and sixpence, a ballot would determine who got the certificate. The process would be repeated until each member got a certificate, and so on. By such ingenious schemes, enormous sums could be raised nationally, and Miss Shaw stated that £250,000 had been raised in this manner in Huddersfield. Wadsworth was eager to participate, followed shortly afterwards by Blackshaw and Erringden who formed a Joint War Savings Committee.

However, such efforts were seemingly not enough, for the government also launched great savings drives, reminiscent of the great recruiting drives of 1914 and 1915. The 'Victory Loan' of February 1917 featured big meetings attended by government representatives who urged the more affluent to seek bank loans or borrow money on their life

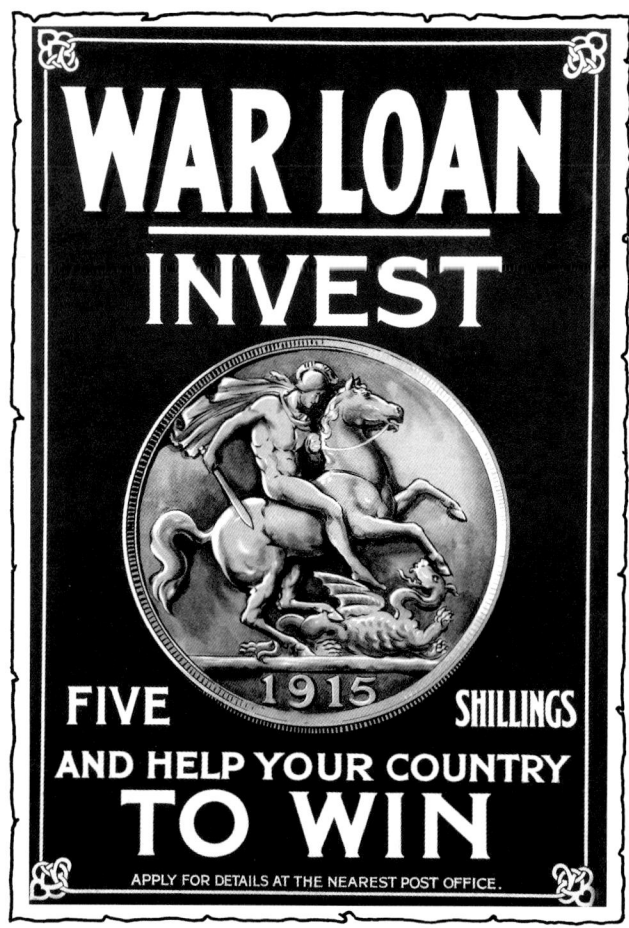

Another great government drive – not for men but for money.

All mediums were used to reinforce the message – words as well as pictures.

insurance policies in order to invest in the 'Victory Loan.'

Also, in response to a call from the Chancellor of the Exchequer in the last week of the drive, all the takings at the Hebden Bridge Co-operative Hall Picture House from the previous Monday and Tuesday evenings were invested in the war loan. Local councils tried to do their patriotic duty, and Mytholmroyd Council put £1,500 into the war loan. This was not to the liking of all, for Councillor Helliwell criticised the decision as an irresponsible use of ratepayers' money.

The 'Victory Loan' drive ended on February 16th 1917. War Savings Certificates were still to be had, and in this respect the Editorial of the *Hebden Bridge District News* carried an uncompromising message. "No-one should dare to squander a single farthing or use up an iota of goods and services on an unnecessary thing. The cry for guns, ammunition, food and clothes for soldiers will grow more and more. The message must be – scrape and scrape!" Such clarion calls were being answered, at every level, for in February 1917 Hebden Bridge National School, reported that in connection with the War Savings Association, the school had experienced a record week, with thirteen pounds and ten shillings being taken. Fund raising depended heavily upon such small amounts being multiplied by wide participation. All West Riding County Council Schools were given a day's holiday in October 1918 to celebrate the raising of £250,000 by Council Schools in War Savings.

Chapter 16 – Money, Money, Money

> **MEANWHILE THE WAR CONTINUES - A YEAR IN THE LIFE...**
>
> *Arnold Thomas was not quite eighteen when he enlisted, with his pal Clement Greenwood, early in December 1917. He threw his egg muffin lunch into the canal outside Central Dyeworks, Hebden Bridge, a symbolic gesture of an old life ending and a new one beginning. In the months to come, there was many a hungry moment when Arnold thought wistfully of that egg muffin slowly sinking into the canal. He was shuffled rapidly through two regiments before embarking to France with the 10th Battalion Essex Regiment. He was wounded twice, his most vivid battlefield memory being of giving a dying officer a drink, only to see the water emerge in a bloody stream from a bullet hole in his throat. Arnold's second wound, a broken jaw inflicted by a bullet, brought him home to hospital in England. The war ended as he was convalescing in Brighton, and he insisted that he had never been so frightened as when the 'jocks' (Scots) rioted there when attempts were made to stop them riding the trains for free.*[8]

Arnold Thomas (left) with older brother Garnet. **A terrible telegram for Arnold's parents to receive.**

---

8 Arnold Thomas was the author's father. A fuller version of his experiences can be found, entitled *The Twentieth Century Remembered: Arnold's Odyssey, 1917- 1918, Transactions of the Halifax Antiquarian Society, Volume 15 New Series, 2007,* pages 122 to 133.

In March 1917, at the Hippodrome in Todmorden, a film was shown entitled *The Battle of Ancre and the Advance of the Tanks*. This was another War Office propaganda film, but was said to be more realistic than *The Battle of the Somme* of the previous year. Clearly the sight of these huge mechanical monsters rumbling across 'no-man's land' captured the public's imagination, for the tank was considered to be a suitable focus for another great savings drive twelve months later. In March 1918, huge excitement was caused in Halifax at the arrival of Egbert the Tank. After a demonstration of manoeuvring at the Shay, Egbert was parked up at Commercial Street to inaugurate 'Tank Bank Week' at Halifax. Thousands turned out to invest in War Savings Certificates under the slogan 'Bank at the Tank.' On the Tuesday, 10,000 or so schoolchildren visited Egbert, some marching from as far away as Wainstalls.

Hebden Bridge had high hopes that Egbert would make its way along the Calder Valley to visit the town, but this was not to be. Hebden Bridge's 'Tank Week' opened on Wednesday, March 20th 1918, but only with a facsimile dummy, described as a 'camouflaged bus tank,' accompanied by a model of the real thing. Nevertheless, intense interest was generated in the district. On the first day, factories and schools were closed and large crowds gathered at the display area, the tram terminus on New Road.

By order of the District Sub-Committee of the W.R.C.C Education Authority, the children & teachers were present in Hebden Bridge from eleven to twelve o'Clock today, to witness the arrival of the War Savings "Tank" & to be present during the inaugural ceremony.

Much excitement for the children of Hebden Bridge National School.

Saturday was perhaps an even more popular day for a visit, and the 'tank' itself took around £1,700 in war savings on that day. Throughout the week there were other outlets for buying War Savings Certificates, including banks and insurance offices, and the final grand total raised by what was officially known as the Hebden Bridge and District War Investment Campaign was the staggering sum of £112,844, representing £9 to £10 per head of population.

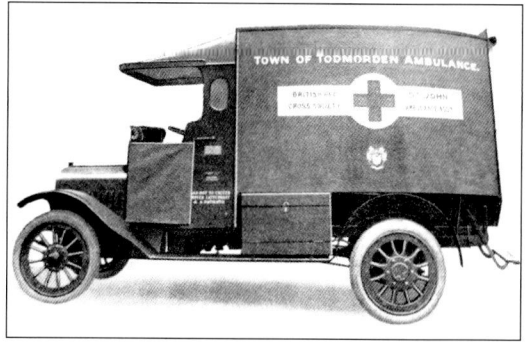

An ambulance for the military provided by Todmorden's money raising efforts.
J.A. Lee

It might be thought that the financial resources of the people of Britain would have been pretty much exhausted by now. Nevertheless another great savings drive was

---

Undoubtedly the highlight of the week was the arrival and installation of a twenty-pounder gun

---

launched in Hebden Bridge in the first week of November 1918. This was 'Feed the Guns Week,' once again part of a nationwide effort. The drive was inaugurated with a film show, *What the Navy has Done*, and a lecture at the Co-operative Hall. Councillor Stansfield was in the chair, and he entreated the people of Hebden Bridge to live up to their reputation of being generous benefactors to such causes. He announced that a good start had been made with a subscription of £10,000 from the Yorkshire Penny Bank.

Undoubtedly the highlight of the week was the arrival and installation of a twenty-pounder gun, accompanied by two army transport wagons, in St. George's Square on Tuesday, November 5th 1918. The gun and vehicles had been painted with customary camouflage design. Entertainment was provided by a military band. Local schoolchildren, no doubt hugely excited, were marched to the event by their teachers, and workshops closed half an hour early. Therefore it was a large crowd which assembled to hear Councillor Stansfield's address from the balcony of the *White Horse*. He admitted that the end of the war was in sight (although he probably did not know that the Armistice was only six days away), but he argued that the guns still needed 'feeding' to finish the job and, "for straightening matters out afterwards." The usual War Savings Certificates were on sale, both at the Council Offices and at the gun itself, but this batch was distinguished with having the shape of a gun stamped on them. 'Feed the Gun Week' raised £109,104.

Apart from investing in the government, there were numerous other ways to support the war effort, financially or otherwise. Funds were always needed, for example, for the upkeep of the two voluntary military hospitals which were operating locally. Centre Vale Military Hospital, at Todmorden, led the way in this respect. From the outset of the war it had been anticipated that the existing hospitals would find it difficult to cope with the flow of military casualties, and auxiliary hospitals sprung up all over the country. The old Centre Vale Mansion

The soldiers enjoyed weekly entertainments provided by local singers and instrumentalists

was utilised as one of these and was largely staffed by volunteer nurses and doctors. Other organisations pitched in to help, including the St. John Ambulance Brigade, the Boy Scouts and members of the V.A.D. (Voluntary Aid Detachment). Most of the furniture, bedding and garments were freely donated.

The first batch of wounded soldiers arrived at Todmorden railway station on November 17th 1914. This was a big event for the town. Private motor cars were put at the disposal of the patients and cheering crowds, including 'released' schoolchildren, lined the route to Centre Vale. The first batch consisted of less severely wounded, but the second batch were all on stretchers, badly wounded and looking haggard and in great pain. The crowds now fell silent as the grim reality of war was brought home to them.

During the first year the Hospital treated 224 patients, including men from Australia, Canada, New Zealand and Russia. Seemingly the people of Todmorden could not do enough for these wounded men, and Christmas 1914 saw them showered with gifts from well-wishers. Hairdressers came in to offer their services free and the local picture houses, the Olympia and the Hippodrome, offered free passes. The soldiers enjoyed weekly entertainments provided by local singers and instrumentalists.

A little girl holds two policemen to ransom in one of Todmorden's money raising drives. J.A. Lee

A well-equipped hospital – owing much to the financial support of the people of Todmorden.
J.A. Lee

Nurses and soldiers at Centre Vale Military Hospital enjoy a little 'time out.'
Courtesy of Stephen Gee

Volunteers, including boy scouts, helped to keep Centre Vale Military Hospital going.
J.A. Lee

Nevertheless, the relationship between the soldiers and the local community occasionally hit a jarring note. The more able of the patients were allowed to go out freely and, in the early days, there were some complaints about rowdy behaviour and drunkenness. At one stage the Mayor of Todmorden, Alderman R. Jackson, issued a warning to the people of Todmorden that their kindness to the invalids must not extend to taking them into their homes and plying them with strong drink. The invalids were still under military regulations and any breach of these could mean the curtailment of the soldiers' liberties.

The Centre Vale Hospital opened with twenty beds, a number which rose steadily to fifty. The Todmorden ratepayers bore the costs of fuel, lighting and water. The staff largely consisted of volunteers and the War Office

---
'Miss Taylor's Little Folk' providing the main entertainment.

---

provided a grant for each patient. However, costs still exceeded income, and extra support had to be provided by a series of money-raising charity events. One of the earliest, a Soldiers' Fete, was held at Centre Vale Park on July 24th 1915, and raised just over £345. The Military Hospital was one of the beneficiaries of a War Charity Concert held in Todmorden. In February 1916, 'Miss Taylor's Little Folk' providing the main entertainment. Summer days provided more opportunities for the utilisation of Centre Vale Park, and in August 1916 a cricket match was held there between convalescent soldiers and a team of former Todmorden First Eleven Players. The latter won an easy victory, but the result was less important than the £50 that was raised for the provision of cigarettes and other comforts for the soldiers. Another £50 was raised later in the year at a rather more high profile charity cricket game at Centre Vale, this time between Todmorden and Walsden, and featuring the cricketing 'giants' of George Hirst and Wilfred Rhodes, (both of Yorkshire and England) as guest players.

Sporadic charity events could only go so far in covering the Hospital's financial deficits. A more regular source of income was needed, and in a way it was the *Hebden Bridge and District News* which put this in motion by setting up its Wounded Soldiers Club. Money was raised from the readership by many means and put into a fund. The first donation to the Hospital came as a result of a bowling match at the *Hare and Hounds*, Todmorden, in August 1916. The soldiers' Cigarettes Fund benefited to the extent of allowing the invalids a packet of five daily. They certainly appreciated this, but supplying comforts to the soldiers was not addressing the problem of the Hospital's upkeep.

A public meeting in September 1916 attempted to come to grips with the problem. The Mayor of Todmorden took the chair and stated that, in spite of private donations and fund raising events, the Hospital would soon would be running into a debit of £80 per month. The most positive step was to issue an appeal in the Public Notices section of the *District News* in December 1916. This asked for donations amounting to £500 to meet the cost of keeping the Hospital going for the next six months. The response was good and included a donation of £50 from Fielden Bros. of Waterside Mill.

The appeal was now repeated on a weekly basis, always accompanied by a list of subscribers and amounts subscribed. In spite of a note of desperation from time to time, such as in March 1917 when it was declared that, "funds are exhausted," these subscriptions, along with other incomes, kept the Hospital floating nicely until the end of the war. In fact, when the Hospital finally closed on February 28th 1919, having treated around 1,000 men in all, the worthy Miss Mabel Eastwood, who had given her services as Honorary Secretary voluntarily throughout the war, published the final account. The closing balance was £763, which was distributed to various local charities, including the St. John Ambulance Brigade and the East Lancashire Homes for Disabled Sailors and Soldiers.

> *Not only did the wounded soldiers at Centre Vale Military Hospital enjoy weekly Saturday evening entertainments, but outings were sometimes laid on for them. On July 29th 1916, Mr Frederick Moss entertained patients at his home, Bridgeroyd House. The more able enjoyed bowls, quoits and tennis in the grounds and refreshments were provided for all. The soldiers arrived by special bus at 2.15 p.m., and left at 8 p.m., having had, "a glorious time."*
>
> *Two visits were made to Cragg Vale in September 1916. The hostess for the first visit was Miss Rigby of Castle Hall, and the catering was provided by Mr James Hartley of the Hinchliffe Arms. The second visit, to Holly House, involved a cricket match between invalids and nurses. The party then progressed to Cragg Hall where Mr and Mrs W.A. Simpson-Hinchliffe laid on, "an excellent meat tea."*

The style of philanthropy initiated at Todmorden became a model for others. Perhaps influenced by the visit to her home of patients from Centre Vale Military Hospital, in September 1916, Miss Rigby of Castle Hall, Cragg Vale, offered part of her house for a similar purpose. This was to be on a smaller scale than the one in Todmorden, providing sixteen beds, and the Castle Hall Military Auxiliary Hospital opened its doors in November 1916, with Miss Rigby in charge. The Hospital was immediately fully occupied with the arrival of sixteen wounded men from St. Luke's Hospital, Halifax. Hebden Bridge would like to have followed suit, and in March 1917 a large and enthusiastic audience at the Victoria Hall adopted the proposal to open a military hospital in the town. A committee was appointed and the Hope Sunday School building was earmarked as a likely place for a hospital. In April, however, Colonel Dunscombe of the military wrote to say that its needs could be better met elsewhere for the moment. With 'cold water' having been poured on the Hebden Bridge scheme, enthusiasm waned and the plans were quietly put aside.

CHAPTER 17 – HELP IN ALL DIRECTIONS

The men in the local military hospitals were rarely local men, and for those whose preference was for charity beginning at home, War Distress Funds or War Relief Committees had sprung to life up and down the Calder Valley from the outset of war. Initially the aim had been the support of the families of serving soldiers if the rather meagre state allowances were causing distress. As the war progressed, and the number of disabled servicemen increased, there was much dissatisfaction at government 'red tape' causing delays in the payment of pensions and allowances to discharged servicemen and their dependents. Believing that self-help might also improve matters, branches of the National Association of Discharged Sailors and Soldiers were formed both in Todmorden and Hebden Bridge in 1917. As was seen in a previous chapter, although their principal aim was to improve the lot of ex-servicemen, their members could also prove to be feisty opponents of any public utterances that they regarded as pacifist.

War Distress Funds in the Upper Calder Valley had widened their scope from late 1914 when Belgian refugees, in need of housing and other assistance, began to enter the locality. If charity was beginning at home it was not ending there, for in May 1916 the Hebden Bridge and District War Distress Committee held a full week of events and collections for the Y.M.C.A., an organisation that was engaged in making life more bearable for soldiers behind the Allied lines in France and elsewhere. Almost £1,000 was raised.

> Other groups were well able to make their own efforts with regard to war charity work, and in January 1916 the Hebden Bridge Amateur Operatic Society, connected with the Hope Baptist Church, had staged a musical operetta to raise funds for what were known as the 'Y.M.C.A. huts' abroad.

Even individuals could make their own personal contribution, in kind if not in cash. The Reverend E.G. Thomas, the pastor at Slack Baptist Church, Heptonstall, was a man with a strong social conscience who believed in translating words into deeds. In late 1917 and early 1918 he exchanged the relative comfort of his vicarage to go and work for four months in a Y.M.C.A. hut in France.

The ever widening scope of the Hebden Bridge and District War Distress Fund was demonstrated in July 1917 when its Committee published the auditors' report. Just over £3,280 had been paid out to support Armenian refugees, relief in Serbia and Poland and to many local organisations. Separate funds had paid out a combined sum of around £2,500 for both the relief of Belgian refugees in England and for the relief of distress in Belgium itself. Similarly, in November 1918, over £6,000 of the £109,104 raised during the Hebden Bridge 'Feed the Guns Week' was permitted to go to the local War Distress Fund.

Members of the local branches of the British Red Cross had been working assiduously throughout the war in collecting and dispatching to the various fronts great quantities of items such as towels, jerseys, shirts, body belts, pyjamas and such like. Anything they could make for themselves they did, for example roller bandages and slings. In the self-help department the Hebden Bridge Red Cross was joined by the War Distress Ladies Sewing Committee, both groups being well able to knit large amounts of mittens, socks and bed socks. All these comforts were for the general good of the Allied Forces, but sometimes the ladies wanted to ensure that local lads got their fair share. Therefore, in November 1916 for example, the Hebden Bridge Red Cross aimed to send two pairs of socks to every man serving from this locality.

The British Red Cross also supported those held in enemy prisoner of war camps by sending parcels whenever possible. However, this was another area where concern for local boys manifested itself in the establishment of a Prisoner of War Fund, sometimes assisted by

WAR HORSE FLAG DAY

In a brutal war, horses and mules suffered hardship, injury and death along with men on the fighting fronts. At a time when so many demands were being made on civilian pockets to support servicemen, the horses were not forgotten. In July 1917 the Society for the Prevention of Cruelty to Animals organised a War Horse Flag Day, in Hebden Bridge, to provide comforts for sick and broken animals engaged in the conflict. Sixty young ladies, helped by a number of boys, spent a Saturday morning selling badges on the streets. Over £80 was raised.

Horses and mules suffered terribly in this war.
Courtesy of Bankfield Museum

the War Distress Fund. In August 1918 local prisoners of war numbered as follows: - Hebden Bridge – eight; Mytholmroyd – two; Heptonstall and Wadsworth – one each. Each of these had received help to the value of around £48.

Wartime Christmases had little enough cheer about them, and inevitably the thoughts of families and friends turned to those who were far away, perhaps enduring Christmas in a cold and wet trench. Local fund raisers tended to concentrate their efforts on 'Soldiers' Christmas Comforts' from each November. Concerts were frequently held to raise money. Nor were the servicemen forgotten at their former places of employment. In mid-December 1917, £15 was collected amongst the workers and directors of the Nutclough Fustian Manufacturing Company, to enable each of the 40 men on the Company's Roll of Honour to receive a postal order for ten shillings. 'Christmas Cheer for the Boys' was the slogan supporting the collection, and similar efforts were made in other local mills.

AN EAR'S BREADTH FROM DEATH

The terrible news for the wife and parents of Ben Collinge of Eton Street, Hebden Bridge, that he had been killed from shrapnel wounds to the throat, was made worse by the fact that he had been expected home on leave. Worse still, Ben's family had recently received a letter describing how he and others had saved the lives of four gunners who had been buried alive under dirt thrown up by an exploding shell. Three had been easy to find. The fourth was seemingly nowhere to be found until Ben spotted an ear sticking out right under his feet. Some frantic digging soon brought the man out alive.

The families of the absent men were not forgotten. The feature concert of Christmas 1916, held at Mytholmroyd Parish Church School, was advertised as a 'Treat for Soldiers' Parents, Wives, Widows and Dependents.' Councillor Thomas Ashton J.P., of Stocks Hall, funded the event, which involved a tea and entertainment. Around 550 people attended the event and this included the wounded men from Castle Hall Military Hospital. Local singers, musicians and

Chapter 17 – Help In All Directions

monologue artistes provided the entertainment, and the Castle Hall soldiers distributed Christmas crackers to the children. These men were themselves absent from home at Christmas, and it was the knowledge that men such as these would also be missing their families that prompted 40 young people from the local Band of Hope Union to visit St. Luke's Hospital, Halifax, in December 1917. The young people performed a children's operetta, *The Compassionate Spirit*, to over 300 invalid soldiers, and their nurses, in the Y.M.C.A. hut stationed in the grounds. The performance was much appreciated by the soldiers, who probably showed equal appreciation of the 2,000 cigarettes, 100 bananas and 70 packets of sweets that were distributed.

Local support for the Belgian refugees had been enormously popular since the enthusiastic reception at Mytholmroyd station of the first batch in November 1914. Accommodation and furniture had been found for them and relief funds set up. With the Belgians in mind, the Mytholmroyd Red Cross, in May 1916, held a 'Cake and Apron White Elephant Stall' which raised around £50 for the cause. This suggests that relations between the locals and the refugees was cordial, but there were bound to be problems for a displaced group of people having left their homes, and virtually everything they owned, behind them in

> *only to be struck in the face by a member of this family*

Belgium. They needed to adapt quickly to a new language and culture, and also to the fact that their economic and social status may well now have been radically different from what they had enjoyed in Belgium.

Nevertheless, whatever problems did come to light seem to have been generated within the Belgian community itself. In August 1917 a special meeting of the Mytholmroyd Distress Committee was convened to discuss the conduct of certain Belgian refugees occupying the Wesleyan Manse. Apparently a dispute had arisen between two of the families occupying the building. In response to complaints about the behaviour of the Vanuxen family, the Chairman of the Distress Committee had visited the Manse only to be struck in the face by a member of this family. The committee agreed that the troublemakers should be cleared out of the Manse, but it was felt that this decision should be made at a higher level.

Another meeting, a week later, only seemed to reflect a worsening situation, with neighbours complaining about the unruliness of Belgian refugees housed at a cottage at Pall Mall, Mytholmroyd. The committee now

> *In December 1917 Miss Lucy Horsfall, of 'Underbank' in Hebden Bridge, was recognised as the official receiver of waste tinfoil for the Hebden Bridge district.*

approached the authorities in London and in only two weeks the log jam of bureaucracy had been cleared away. Furnished with rail passes and photographs the troublesome Belgians, nine in all, departed by train for London in September 1917, apparently very willing to go.

Meanwhile local people continued to make heroic efforts to help the war effort in one way or another, and this could take some surprising forms. In December 1917 Miss Lucy Horsfall, of 'Underbank' in Hebden Bridge, was recognised as the official receiver of waste tinfoil for the Hebden Bridge district. The remit was wide, including the wrappings of tea, cigarettes, tobacco, sweetmeats and tangerines; capsules of bottles and jars; and even paint and other old lead. Miss Horsfall's record was impressive, having accumulated one and a quarter hundredweight of waste tinfoil between March and September 1917, and its sale had released £6:14 shillings, the cash being shared between Centre Vale Hospital, Castle Hall Hospital and the local Red Cross.

Waste paper was another prime target for local salvage operations. One of the earliest indicators of paper problems came in the *Hebden Bridge and District News* for April 7th 1916. The editor announced that the newspaper would have to be reduced in size by roughly one third, giving as his reasons that the import of wood pulp for paper-making had been reduced by a third due to government demands on shipping, and the cost of paper had doubled. This was followed by an appeal for people to economise with respect to paper. Perhaps galvanised by this appeal, along with the national appeal embodied in the establishment of the Prince of Wales' Waste Newspaper Fund, local schoolchildren set to with a will. In the next six months, by dint of collecting and bringing in bundles of old newspapers and magazines to their schools, local children amassed over a ton of paper. Its sale realised £6 : 6 shillings, which was sent to the Prince of Wales' Fund.

In this same month, October 1916, the military authorities in the West Riding of Yorkshire, banned 'Gunpowder Plot' bonfires. The fact that fireworks were sanctioned, apart from rockets, suggests that both bonfires and rockets were regarded as a possible means of signalling messages to the enemy. However, the dual purpose was also served of preserving potential bonfire wood for making paper. Nevertheless, as late as January 1918, Lord Rhondda was still complaining that his appeal of twelve months earlier for local authorities to take responsibility for waste paper collection, and put it on a systematic basis, had met with poor results. Sadly, Hebden Bridge district was one of the areas where nothing 'official' had been done.

> *In some cases waste became not only unpatriotic but even illegal. In August 1918 Sarah Schofield of Bar Street, Todmorden, was summoned before the local magistrates under the Waste of Foodstuffs Order (1918). It was alleged that the previous month, just prior to going on holiday with her husband, "she threw half a loaf of bread into the waste bucket." How this misdemeanour came to light was not revealed, but in consequence she was fined £1. The Food Control Committee, which had brought the charge, did not press for a heavier fine but wanted this case, the first of its kind in the district, to be seen as a warning to others.*

Under-utilised man-power was also regarded as a kind of waste. If men could not for any reason serve in the armed forces, they

German invasion scares never entirely disappeared

must contribute to the defence of Britain in other ways, and not just through war work. There was felt to be a very real need for home defence, for even after the first German attacks in the West in 1914 had been repelled, and the trench stalemate established, German invasion scares never entirely disappeared. As a result the setting up of Voluntary Training Corps (V.T.C.) units was encouraged in every urban or rural district – the forerunners of Local Defence Volunteers, or Home Guard, of the Second World War. Volunteers tended to be men exempted from conscription or men too old, too young or too unfit to join the regulars and territorials. In no way was it intended as a safe haven for potential fighting men.

In October 1916, Hebden Bridge formed a unit of the V.T.C. – platoon 12 of the 8th Battalion (Halifax) of the West Riding Volunteers. Mytholmroyd followed suit a week later, both units numbering about 50 each. As a larger borough, Todmorden was able to boast a membership of around 150 in 1916. V.T.C. units, meeting at evenings and weekends, spent their time in drilling, marching and weapons training. One high spot must have been the participation of local units in the weekend inspection of 30,000 Volunteers from the North of England by the nationally known figure of Field Marshall Viscount French. This took place in December 1916 at the Knavesmire, York, and mingled with the praise of Viscount French, was an apology for the shortage of arms and equipment for the V.T.C. – a problem which was to dog the Home Guard in World War Two. Such shortages seemingly did not blunt the enthusiasm shown by the Hebden Bridge and Mytholmroyd Units in their engagement in a 'sham battle,' fought on Norland Moor, just before Christmas 1916. This was a large scale affair, involving the Halifax and Huddersfield Battalions, with 400 on one side and 500 on the other.

Chapter 17 – Help In All Directions

> **MEANWHILE AT THE FRONT - UNEXPECTED INJURIES**
>
> *Private Gerald Horsfall, formerly a hairdresser of Mytholmroyd, may have expected many things when he departed for France, but not to have all his toes amputated. This had to be done in April 1917 after he had contracted 'trench foot,' a condition which resulted from prolonged exposure of the feet to mud and water.*
>
> *Similarly, Driver J.W. Speak of Earnshaw Water, Blackshaw, may have expected injury from the enemy, but not from a horse. However, whilst in France he was severely bitten in the face by a horse.*
>
> *It was a pointer to new technology and the future when Private W.I. Stansfield, of Hebden Bridge, was killed in France by an aeroplane bullet in September 1918.*

Although the V.T.C. was essentially a voluntary organisation, the tone adopted by some Military Tribunals was that men granted exemption from conscription ought to join the V.T.C. (or sometimes take up an allotment). In some cases Tribunals were pointing to membership of the V.T.C. as a *condition* of exemption. There was some unease at this, often expressed in the local press, and its legality was questioned. However, matters were put on a legal footing by the Military Service Act (No.2), which stated that men exempted after April 3rd 1918 were required to join their local V.T.C. unit and attend for no less than 12 hours per week. If this seems clear cut, apparently it wasn't. In September 1918 the editor of the *Hebden Bridge and District News* wondered why a man holding an 'exemption certificate' had to join the V.T.C.; whilst a man holding a 'protection certificate' had neither to do military service nor join the V.T.C. In his wonderment, the editor simply states, "It passes our comprehension."

The men who joined the V.T.C. probably did so with feelings that fell somewhere on a scale between reluctance and enthusiasm. There was little of the latter shown, however, when the government attempted to promote its National Service Scheme in March 1917. A spokesman gave a talk on this matter in Todmorden Town Hall, stating that anybody who registered with the scheme could stay in his or her old employment, but had to be willing to be moved wherever needed, "in the national interest." An employer could object, in which case, a government committee would decide. A similar scheme was already in place for munitions, but the emphasis on the new plan seemed to be on agriculture, particularly ploughing.

> MEN, country born and country bred, now engaged in the cities; amateur gardeners, professional gardeners, flower growers, brickyard hands, livery stablemen, road menders, water-pipe layers, golf club employees, outdoor servants, gamekeepers, hedgers and ditchers, and, above all, ex-ploughmen and men who have worked on the land—OFFER YOUR SERVICES during these critical months.
>
> *"The farmers could increase even now by hundreds of thousands of tons the food of this country this year. One of the main obstacles is lack of labour."* Mr. LLOYD GEORGE.
>
> **ENROL TO-DAY**
> **For National Service**
> And help to defeat the Grimmest Menace that ever threatened this Country

Food supplies were a major problem by 1917.

Much debate and dispute followed this presentation at the Todmorden Town Hall, but much of the audience was somewhat nonplussed at the government's request. How could this be done, asked one questioner, when machines in the local cotton trade were lying idle for want of labour? This lukewarm response was duplicated at a council meeting in Hebden Bridge where, as in Todmorden, employers were desperately trying to save their men from conscription. It was thought that no man could be spared and hence no action was to be taken.

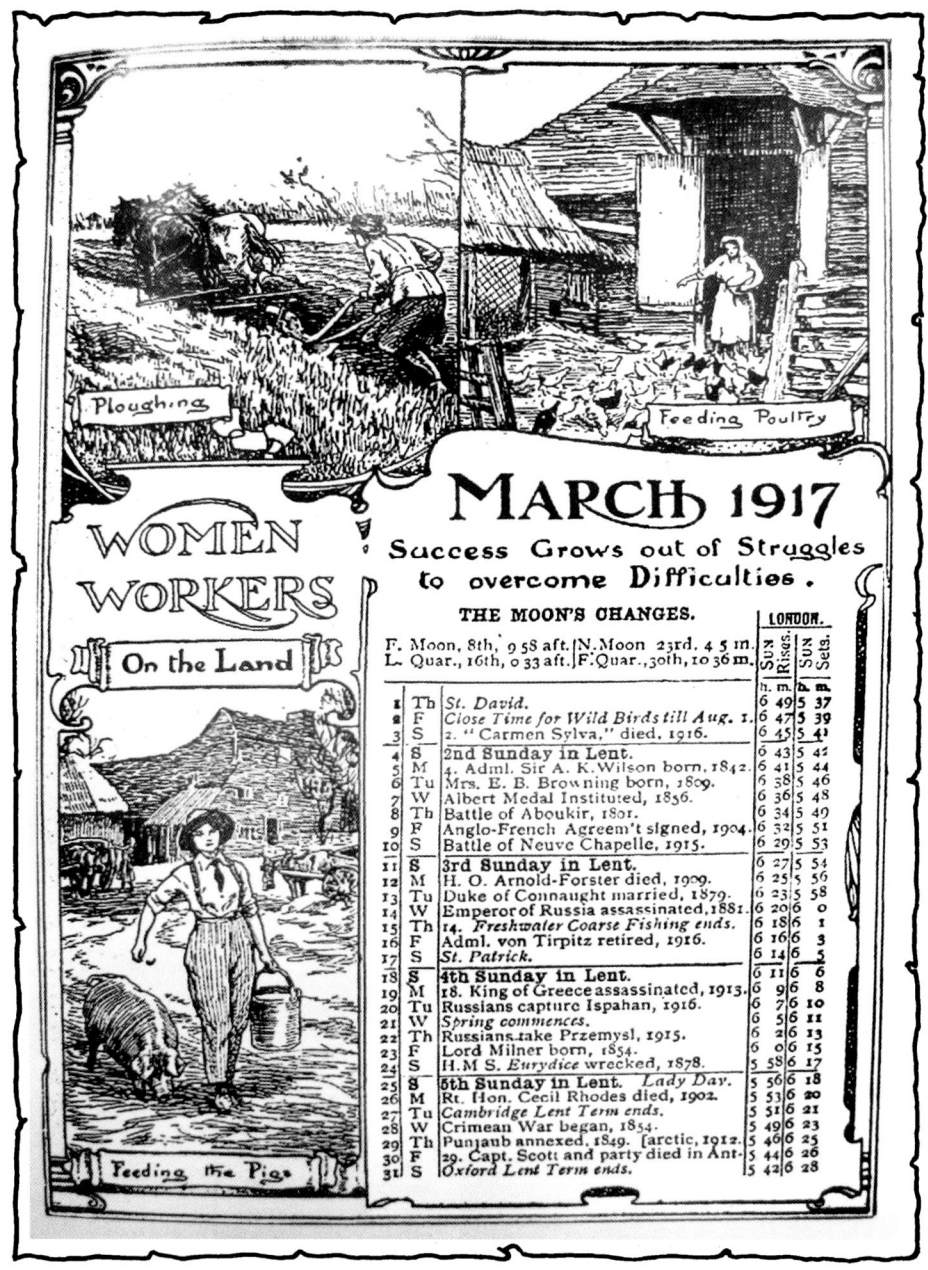

The Land Girls get stuck into 'men's' jobs. Notice the military tone of the calendar.
Halifax Guardian Historical Almanack

CHAPTER 18 – THE BITTER END

At the beginning of 1918, few people could have predicted with confidence when the war was going to end, or even the likely winner. The deadlock on the Western Front held fast. Nevertheless the year 1917 had seen 'straws in the wind,' hints that the following year might be one of huge changes. Russia had been convulsed by two revolutions, the result being the establishment of a Bolshevik government under Lenin, a government which at the very least could be regarded as unpredictable. In April 1917 the German return to unrestricted submarine warfare finally brought the U.S.A. into the war on the side of the Allies. The power and almost limitless resources of this nation would surely make a difference, but how long would it take for the U.S.A. to fully gear up for war and get trained troops across to Europe in significant numbers?

Far too long in the eyes of Ludendorff, Germany's Commander-in-Chief. Russia went out of the war with the signing of the Treaty of Brest-Litovsk early in March 1918. With hundreds of thousands of German troops now able to be transferred from the Eastern to the Western Front, Ludendorff reckoned that his revitalised German forces would be able to deliver a knockout blow before the American soldiers could really get into the war. Hence Operation Michael, a massive German attack on the Somme which began on March 21st 1918.

Within a few days the Germans had advanced forty miles, and defeat seemed to be staring the Allies in the face. However, the British and French lines bulged but did not break. Ludendorff overstretched himself and supplies to his troops became a problem. With every day that the Allies held out, more American troops poured into France.

> Pte. J. G. Berkley, Northumberland Fusiliers, of Commercial Street, Hebden Bridge, writer of several entertaining letters which have been published in this paper, has been gassed—not seriously, we are glad to state.
>
> Pte. E. Pickles, Royal Scots, of 11, Barker's Terrace, Hebden Bridge, has been brought to the Southern General Hospital, Birmingham, following an operation in hospital at Etaples for gunshot wound in the left arm.
>
> Sgt. Alec Blackie, of Balmoral Street, Hebden Bridge, has been severely wounded in the head, and the skull is fractured.
>
> Pte. Frank Greenwood, son of Mr. Pilling Greenwood, Queen's Terrace, Hebden Bridge, has been wounded in France, and is in hospital at Boulogne. This is the second time he has been wounded. He went out with the First Fourths in April, 1915.
>
> Second-Lieutenant Harold Sutcliffe, R.F.A., elder son of the late Mr. W. H. Sutcliffe, solicitor, and Mrs. Sutcliffe, of Brearley House, is in Alexandra Park Military Hospital, Stockport, suffering from shell-gas poisoning. Ten other officers, including the Colonel of his Brigade, were also gassed in the recent heavy fighting in France. Gunner Holt, of Upper Lee, Hebden Bridge, in the same Battery as Lieut. Sutcliffe, is also in hospital, gassed.
>
> Sergeant Walter Butterworth, Royal Fusiliers, of Wiod End, Hebden Bridge, was recently gassed, but has recovered and has rejoined his battalion.
>
> Pte. James Greenwood, of Popples Side, Heptonstall, formerly grocery manager for the Heptonstall Co-operative Society, has been invalided to England, and since transferred to a Scottish hospital, suffering from the effects of shell gas.
>
> Pte. Arthur Smith, East Yorkshire Regiment, son of Mr. and Mrs. Alfred Smith, 17, Milner Royd, Luddenden Foot was wounded on the 22nd March. No details are given in the communication. Pte. Smith joined the Army in the early stages of the war, and has seen much active service. This is the second time he has been wounded. He is 24 years old, and was formerly employed at Fairlea Mill. Both he and his brother William (also serving) are well known as local Association football players.
>
> Gunner J. P. Waddington, R.G.A., of Pleasant View, Hebden Bridge, has been wounded on the ankle, and is in the 7th Canadian Stationary Hospital, France.
>
> Pte. Willie Pickles, Higher Edgehey Green, is reported wounded.
>
> Pte. Ira Speak, of Slack Top, has been wounded.

The last big campaigns caused 1918 to be a catastrophic year for casualties.

> On August 8th 1918 General Haig launched a British counter attack near Amiens. The French followed suit, and from this point the Allied advance never ceased. The fighting was bitter, however, and 1918 exceeded any other year in terms of total casualties.

A German defeat by the end of the year still seemed unlikely to the leading Allied politicians and generals. However, German resistance collapsed in November 1918. Her allies had fallen away; Kaiser Wilhelm II abdicated on November 9th; faced with imminent revolution amongst a starving population, a delegation from the newly formed republic agreed to an Armistice. The cease fire began at 11 a.m. on November 11th, the final acts in the drama having come so quickly that many were taken by surprise.

This seems to have been the case locally. On the morning of the Armistice rumours were abroad in Hebden Bridge, but by 11.20 a.m. excited conjecture had become official news. Mills and businesses closed down at once and the streets were soon filled with a jubilant throng of people. Schools closed in the early afternoon and the children were awarded a day's holiday for the following Friday, November 15th. Belgian refugees joined the party and the strains of the 'Marseillaise' could be heard in the streets. Flags and bunting appeared; the Hebden Bridge Brass Band played in front of the council offices; for the first time since the outbreak of war, the bells of Heptonstall Church came floating down the hillside. Such scenes were replicated in Mytholmroyd and Luddenden Foot. Fireworks even made an appearance up and down the Calder Valley, although strictly speaking these should have been sanctioned by the police. Street and shop window lighting restrictions were partly lifted at once, but not fully because there was still a shortage of coal.

> *Todmorden had an interesting variation on the celebrations. The owners of Mons Mill gave every one of their 420 employees a £1 bank note, honouring an old promise that this would be done when the town of Mons was retaken from the enemy. Mons was recaptured on November 11th, just a few hours before the Armistice.*

Not everyone could share in the seemingly unrestrained joy of Armistice Day. Victory had been bought at huge human cost, and for the families which had suffered the loss of one or more of their menfolk the all-pervading atmosphere must have been sadness. Some of these families would have known exactly the fate of their loved ones. For others, the information passed to them would have been no more than, "missing, presumed dead." Over forty percent of the men killed in the Great War had no known grave. The *Hebden Bridge Times* showed its sensitivity to the more sombre side

---
In June 1918 an influenza epidemic had struck Britain

---

of the occasion when it prefaced its description of the celebrations surrounding Armistice Day by an appeal to its readers to remember, "the many men who have made the supreme sacrifice in securing this long-desired day, and who will never come back again."

There was, in any case, another enemy to be defeated, an insidious one that could prove just as deadly as a German shell or bullet. In June 1918 an influenza epidemic had struck Britain. Although entitled 'Spanish flu,' or the 'Spanish Lady,' it is said to have originated in army camps in the U.S.A., being then brought to Europe by soldiers. In July, 700 Londoners died in one week. After a short abatement, the 'flu' returned more virulently in autumn, killing 18,000 Londoners.

This pattern was reflected locally. A report in the press, dated July 5th 1918, stated that the numbers affected by the outbreak of the 'flu' in

> *the war had reduced the number of Hebden Bridge doctors to two*

the previous month, "has now grown to a considerable magnitude." Schools and workshops were experiencing absences, and because the demands of the war had reduced the number of Hebden Bridge doctors to two, they were being kept very busy. Nevertheless, there had been no fatalities up to this point. In late October, however, the clerk to the local council was declaring that there did not appear to be too much 'flu' in the district.

By mid-November it was all change again. 'Flu' was back with a vengeance. Stubbings Council School was closed for a week because all but one of the staff was down with the illness. The log book of Hebden Bridge National School records that the school was so ravaged by influenza that on November 19th, by the order of the Medical Officer and the sanitary authority, the school was to close for two weeks. This stretched to three weeks in the end, almost to the brink of the Christmas holidays – a great time for those children well enough to enjoy it!

The influenza epidemic hit Hebden Bridge National School hard, causing it to close for three weeks.

Therefore at a time when the people of Britain were trying to come to terms with the casualties of war, the random visitations of disease were inflicted upon them. It is estimated that up to 230,000 died in Britain by the time that this particular horror faded away in the spring of 1919. Local opinion felt that this area was fortunate in that it experienced a less virulent form of the disease than was experienced in some parts of the country. Before 1918 came to a close, however, there was at least one local fatality. Fred. Helliwell, a

> **THE IRONIES OF WAR**
> *Formerly a railway porter at Todmorden station, Corporal David Watt (Scots Guards) was engaged in the war from its outset. He was back in Todmorden in September 1914, being the first local man to have been reported wounded – at Mons the previous month. He was wounded twice more by the end of 1916. In August 1918 he was gassed so badly that he never entirely recovered and he was 'demobbed' in December. David Watt had been a survivor. Close to death on more than one occasion, he had got through from 1914 to the end. He returned to work in January 1919 and died from 'Spanish flu' a fortnight later.*

teenager living at White Houses, Mytholmroyd, was well enough to do a full morning's work on Saturday, November 16th. In the afternoon, he was preparing to join his pals in the Wesley Company of the Boy Scouts, when a slight cold suddenly became bad enough for his mother to pack him off to bed. He quickly deteriorated and never rose from his bed, dying in the early hours of Monday morning. What was perhaps most shocking was the speed with which Spanish 'flu' claimed Fred Helliwell's life, a typical feature of the disease.

Armistice Day, then, did not completely remove all worries from the minds of civilians, but there was still the return of the servicemen to look forward to. In the meantime the district experienced a small exodus as the Belgian refugees left for home. Fourteen Belgian families who had been housed in Hebden Bridge left on February 21st 1919. The local War Relief Committee arranged for their transport to Hull. The uncertainty of the situation in France and Belgium accounted for the delay.

An even greater lapse of time affected demobilisation and 'uncertainty' was again the explanation. The government's thinking was that the Armistice was not a peace treaty. In theory Germany could have recommenced fighting if its government had rejected the

"lies, damned lies and demobilisation lies."

Armistice terms. Therefore many British servicemen were obliged to stay abroad in uniform, probably not knowing why. Unrest grew in the winter of 1918-1919, when soldiers suspected that they were being fed, "lies, damned lies and demobilisation lies." In some towns where soldiers were based there were riots. Nevertheless, ten months after the Armistice there were still a million men in uniform.

The ones who got home quicker were the wounded and prisoners of war. Throughout the conflict, letters home had contained mixed messages about the treatment of local prisoners of war. Officers were allowed to make a financial contribution to ease their living conditions. Men from the ranks, however, were at the mercy of their captors. A letter in June 1915, from Private T.A. Sutcliffe of Wood End, Hebden Bridge, states that he was not being badly treated. In September 1915, an even more positive note was struck by John William Sunderland of Broughton Street, Hebden Bridge. Having been severely wounded, "in the lower extremities," his cheerful letter home claims that he was being treated very well. He was receiving fruit, cocoa and a bottle of beer or stout daily, and he even had access to a gramophone. However, he was in a German hospital, where conditions were likely to have been better than in a camp.

The Turks emerged from the war with a bad reputation in terms of prisoner treatment in some parts of their empire, but Private S. Sutcliffe of Gledhill Street, Todmorden, taken prisoner at Gallipoli in 1915, wrote of them as, "humane captors."

Of course letter writers may have felt the need to be a little careful as to what they wrote, but when John Breeze arrived home in Midgley in 1915, on a prisoner exchange scheme, he felt able to talk freely, giving a vivid account of his experiences which reflected badly on the Germans. Having been wounded near Ypres, he and others lay in a hut on the battlefield with little food and no water. At one point, some Germans stormed into the hut and shot at prisoners. Eventually he was transferred to a hospital and fitted with a wooden leg. However, his only food was chestnut soup and boiled tapioca, and John was convinced that had he been treated earlier he would never have needed to lose his leg.

Good treatment or otherwise of prisoners depended partly on the humanity of the captors and partly on conditions. The latter radically worsened in Germany in 1918. In the first place the number of Allied prisoners jumped sharply during the big German offensive of spring 1918. In the March of that year, for example, there were 21 Todmorden men in captivity. By November this number had shot up to over 100. The problem of many more mouths to feed was compounded by the deteriorating economic situation in Germany. The British naval blockade of German ports had plunged the country into a food crisis by 1918. Deprived of imports, the German people faced widespread starvation, especially in the cities. It has been calculated that more people died of starvation in Germany in this war than were killed in the Allied bombing campaign of the Second World War. In these circumstances prisoners of war probably came at the bottom of the list in terms of food distribution. These factors partly explain some of the terrible stories told by returning local prisoners of war towards the end of 1918, but clearly there was some needless brutality exercised upon them as well.

Sam Crossley, aged 19, returned to his home at the *White Swan*, Hebden Bridge, with a graphic description of his privations. He and his fellow prisoners had been forced into doing heavy work such as quarrying and trench digging. At the slightest pretext the Uhlan guards had delivered kicks and blows. The diet was miserable – a tiny portion of bread daily, supplemented by a bowl of soup that was unsurprisingly very weak since only ten cabbages were used to produce soup for about 600 men. The ever hungry prisoners had to resort to boiling dandelion leaves to provide a little extra sustenance. To their eternal credit, the civilian inhabitants of a nearby village (probably with little enough to eat themselves) sometimes threw bread over the camp fence. If the guards spotted this, however, they would drive the prisoners away and trample the bread into the ground.

> ### IN CAPTIVITY
>
> *<u>Ralph Sutcliffe</u>: Back home in Osborne Street, Hebden Bridge, after being a prisoner since May 1918, he revealed scars on his legs made by the dogs which his captors had set on him. He stated that the prisoners, "generally were cruelly treated."*
>
> *<u>Albert Potentier</u> : Formerly of Hebden Bridge, and visiting relatives here, Albert had been a prisoner since April 1915, during which time he had lost three stones in weight. His refusal to work meant that he had been harshly punished, but in his view the treatment of all the prisoners was, "most abominable."*
>
> *<u>Harold Farrar</u> : After being taken prisoner in March 1918, he had to work in a coal mine. Food was short and men had to do this heavy work until they dropped from exhaustion.*

CHAPTER 19 – A TIME TO REFLECT

So, how to pay tribute to all those who had donned uniform to participate in the greatest war the world had ever seen – those who were returning and those who were not – including

> *By November 30th 1915, a fund of £250 had been raised in Todmorden to enable gold watches to be presented to medal winners.*

ambulance men and nurses? One issue that was already ongoing was that of honours and distinctions. Throughout the war, men from the Upper Calder Valley had won medals for bravery, sometimes the D.C.M. (Distinguished Conduct Medal), more commonly the M.M. (Military Medal), for men from the ranks. By November 30th 1915, a fund of £250 had been raised in Todmorden to enable gold watches to be presented to medal winners. On that day, five Todmorden D.C.M. winners were presented with their watches at the Town Hall. More ceremonies of this kind followed at intervals. On August 31st 1917, for example, the Mayor of Todmorden presented gold watches to four M.M. winners – Sergeant Harry Waller, his brother Corporal Fred Waller, and Privates J.E. Fielden and Arthur Marshall. By the time 'Peace Day' was reached in summer 1919, 69 Todmorden men had received a watch, each with his name inscribed on it.

Further down the valley, on October 26th 1917, a packed room at St. Michael's Sunday School, Mytholmroyd, warmly applauded as a gold watch was presented to Corporal Harold W. Thomas of Albert Street, Mytholmroyd, in recognition of his winning the M.M., "for bravery under fire." Yet again, at Luddenden in June 1918, medal winner Private Harold Naylor Helliwell, was presented with a gold watch, paid for out of a fund established in Luddenden and Midgley.

Sadly, Hebden Bridge was a conspicuous absentee in this particular field. It was not as if

Charles Landale – the first Hebden Bridge man to be awarded a medal for gallantry – the Distinguished Conduct Medal (D.C.M.)

Courtesy of Pennine Horizons

Hebden Bridge did not have its share of medal winners. Corporal Charles Landale, for example, of King Street in Hebden Bridge, won the D.C.M. for connecting signal wires whilst under heavy fire. Not only this, a Hebden Bridge and District War Honours Fund was set up in December 1917 in order to recognise, in practical form, the achievements of those men who had won honours and distinctions. The Fund relied on public subscriptions, but by June 1918 it was clear that not enough had been forthcoming. Valiant efforts were being made, however. In May, Miss Platt of King Street, Hebden Bridge, had composed a hymn tune, 'Fortitude,' copies of which were sold in local workshops, at 1d a time, all proceeds to go to the War Honours Fund. In June, the 12th Platoon of the Volunteer Training Corps held a gala day on Calder Holmes which raised over £156 in aid of the Fund. The whole endeavour sank to anti-climax in November 1918, when the War Honours Committee declared that it could not obtain a supply of watches for presentation due to, "the state of trade." By Armistice Day, then, the Hebden Bridge scheme had ground to a halt.

> *An unusual gesture of recognition for wartime services was the well-deserved one received by Mrs A.F. Thomas of Machpelah, Hebden Bridge. In July 1918, H.M. King of the Belgians conferred upon her the Medaille de la Reine Elisabeth for her assistance to Belgian refugees and soldiers.*

Most soldiers received the Allied Victory Medal (left) and the British War Medal (right) for service in a theatre of war.

3/12759, PRIVATE, Arnold Royston RILEY

8th Battalion.
Duke of Wellington's (West Riding Regiment)
Killed in action, France & Flanders, 29/09/16
Born: Halifax, Enlisted: Derby, Residence: Hebden Bridge, Yorks

Such scrolls were presented to the next of kin of the fallen.
Courtesy of Peter Robertshaw

The majority of men, however, had not won special medals and honours. They had simply done their duty, and they received recognition in the shape of two awards – the British War Medal and the Victory Medal. In the months and years that followed, war memorials and rolls of honour came into being throughout the district. The names on them sometimes listed all that had served from a particular district, or institution, sometimes only the fallen. With regard to the latter, the names of men who died up to 1921 were included if it was thought that their deaths were attributable to their military service. The definition of 'local men' was often generous, for the names of men who had left the district but whose families still lived locally were often included. There were other liberal interpretations of 'local'.

Churches and chapels set up memorials to the men connected with them, sometimes in the grounds, sometimes inside with plaques and rolls of honour or books of remembrance. Even the odd piece of stained glass appeared, as at Luddenden St. Mary's with the names of 19 dead inscribed. Factories, sporting clubs, working men's clubs and schools sometimes created memorials, as did the St. John Ambulance Brigade.

CHAPTER 19 – A TIME TO REFLECT

All manner of organisations created their own tributes.

Courtesy of Stuart Greenwood

The unveiling of memorials was always a solemn and sometimes elaborate ceremony. The one at Mount Zion Baptist Church, Heptonstall Slack, was given generous treatment in the local press. Taking place on August 31st 1919, the memorial listed 44 names of men from the Church and Sunday School who had served. Seven of these had died, and the words, 'In Memoriam' were attached to their names. At a more intimate level, the Young People's Society of the Eastwood Congregational Church and School had set up a Comforts Committee during the war in order to assist servicemen connected with the above. After the war, as a tribute, these young people created a Historical Album (1914-1920),[9] giving pen pictures of each man's war experiences, with photographs attached wherever possible. They did not hesitate to include the biography of a notable conscientious objector, Mr J.W. Thomas.

The creation of public memorials with a list of names of all the men from a particular district or township proved to be problematic. These depended on public subscriptions and/or generous private donations. Luddenden and Midgley were provided with a combined one; Luddenden Foot had its own. Smeakin Hill, below

Memorial plaque in St. James' Church, Hebden Bridge.
Louise Thomas

Pecket Well, was the site of a miniature Stoodley Pike upon which were inscribed the names of 34 men from the parish of Wadsworth who lost their lives.

Elsewhere, a quite impressive war memorial was unveiled at Mytholmroyd in July 1922, but without names on it. As for Hebden Bridge, it was a rather sorry story. There was much earnest discussion in the early months of 1919, and the idea of a memorial cottage hospital received much support. Having discarded this idea, however, the Memorial

Heptonstall Wesleyan Methodist Church memorial plaque.
Louise Thomas

---

9 This fascinating document can be accessed at
http://www.hebdenbridgehistory.org.uk/charlestown/eastwood/eastwoodalbum.html.

Chapter 19 – A Time To Reflect

The memorial at Luddenden to the fallen of Luddenden and Midgley. Louise Thomas

All these memorials were tangible evidence of the effects of war. The mental and emotional impact on those who toiled on the Home Front, and those who returned from the fighting fronts, must have covered every variation. This particularly applied to the returning servicemen, many of whom suffered from either physical or mental injury, or both, this at a time when post-conflict trauma was unrecognised, even though 'shell-shock' (rather grudgingly) had been. Many returning men simply remained silent as to the horrors they had witnessed.

Therefore it is strange to receive the impression that nothing had changed when reading the *Hebden Bridge Times* of late 1918. As in 1914, complaints are made about the price of milk; angry letters are exchanged between the pro-temperance and anti-temperance lobbies. And yet – the Austro-Hungarian and Ottoman Empires

"the bright and promising lives lost to their kindred and country."

had collapsed; the Kaiser had abdicated; Russia was in turmoil; over ten million were dead. The letters in the newspaper may have suggested 'no change,' but the editor was in no doubt as to the magnitude of what was going on. With each passing year the 'retrospectives' struck an increasingly melancholy note.

Committee was still discussing alternatives in 1924. The cost of a garden and cenotaph seemed to be the sticking point and, rather shamefully, the Committee allowed the whole idea to fade away. It was not until August 1938 (on the brink of another world war) that £5,000 was publicly subscribed to open the Memorial Gardens on New Road. The small memorial enclosed within was, to say the least, a modest effort. In total contrast, with perhaps the shadow of Gallipoli still hanging over them, the people and businessmen of Todmorden raised £13,500 in one month in order to create a worthy memorial to their fallen. The magnificent Garden of Remembrance, in Centre Vale Park, contained statuary and 24 tablets of Portland stone with names inscribed. Around 15,000 people attended its opening on October 9th 1921.

The rather disappointing memorial in the park at New Road, Hebden Bridge. Louise Thomas

Part of the Roll of Honour that once could be found at Hope Baptist Church, Hebden Bridge.

Courtesy of Peter Robertshaw

The review of 1917 had commented that no week had passed by without sad news and lamented, "the bright and promising lives lost to their kindred and country." The editor went on to liken this sacrifice to that of Jesus Christ in that these young men had been fighting to rid the world of an evil – that of militarism. Finally he urged the bereaved, "to be courageous, hopeful and enduring." Not even this morsel of encouragement could be found in the editorial retrospective of 1918. It simply stated that the year had been the costliest of the war in terms of lives, with over 100 men from Hebden Bridge and district dying, "bringing the total death roll roughly up to 300."

Depending on how the editor interpreted 'Hebden Bridge and district,' this proved to be a conservative estimate. In compiling his monumental 'Hebden Bridge and District Roll of Honour,' local historian Mike Edwards has put the figure at 417, the area covered being Blackshawhead, Heptonstall, Erringden, Hebden Bridge, Wadsworth, and Mytholmroyd. Some men lost from Midgley, Luddenden and Luddenden Foot appear in the 'Roll of Honour,' but around 95 further names can be found on the two memorials erected in those districts. This provides a total of 512 men. However, this can only be a rough total, as the calculation of war deaths in any area is not a precise science.

One way or another Britain had got through this terrible conflict with its unity more or less intact. The strains on this unity at a local level probably reflected the national picture. From the outset, local trades unionists and the Independent Labour Party condemned profiteering and, as food supplies diminished and prices increased, demanded government control and rationing in the name of equality. This belatedly came. Another fracture line was the recruiting campaign and the perceived issue of 'shirkers'. Conscription, in seemingly solving this problem, created another in the

Chapter 19 – A Time To Reflect

Peace Day at Mytholmroyd – July 1919. Tom Morgan, Mount Zion lay preacher, addresses the crowd.
Courtesy of Peter Robertshaw

suspicion that the Military Tribunals which judged exemption appeals unduly favoured upper and middle class applicants.

Nevertheless there was one binding influence which overcame these strains and stresses and promoted unity. This was the conviction that this was a just war against unbridled German militarism. Not only this, the majority of sermons in churches and chapels preached that this was a Christian war being waged against the forces of darkness. Therefore conscientious objectors, who seemed to deny this principle, received scant public support. In the same vein, as more lives were lost, pacifism, which called for an early end to the war and a 'just peace,' seemed to imply that these lives had been lost in vain. As a result it was no match for government propaganda, or vocal pressure groups, which demanded the utter and complete defeat of Germany.

In June 1919, with peace virtually assured by the imminent signing of the Treaty of Versailles, a Thanksgiving Sunday was observed by religious institutions throughout the land. Also, Saturday July 19th 1919 was set aside for nationwide peace festivities. Following on from these came the unveiling of the Cenotaph in London, the solemn return of the Unknown Soldier, the symbolic adoption of the poppy and the two minutes nationwide silence annually at 11a.m. on November 11th.

All these were tributes and memorials to the fallen, but in looking back in this way people were bound to ask the question 'why?' There was a general feeling that never again should nations blindly rush into war, at such enormous cost. As a result the proposal in 1918 of the President of the U.S.A., Woodrow Wilson, that a League of Nations should be set up to try and forestall all future conflicts, was widely supported. Shortly after Armistice Day, local religious leaders called a public meeting at the Co-operative Hall, Hebden Bridge, to discuss the proposal. Therefore amidst the grieving and the bitterness, this was a chance to look forward. With hindsight we know that the following two decades were merely an interlude between two great wars, but without optimism what hope was there for anyone in 1918 to create something positive out of the Great War?

There was hope too that a future generation would do better. This book began with the death of a young soldier, Robert Arnold Thomas, in a Manchester hospital. In November 1918 his older brother, James, inscribed a tribute to him on the flyleaf of his Lord Wharton Bible. Later, in 1920, James wrote something further, at the back of his Bible, which read as follows,

"Our Son,
    Robert Hopkinson Thomas,
    Born Wednesday May 26th 1920,
    May God bless him and give
    him health and strength to
    fight life's battles.
    His Dad, May 30th 1920."

Robert Hopkinson Thomas received his first name in honour of his uncle and as a link with a tragedy of the past. The rest of the inscription contained a hope for the future. It remained to be seen whether the nation could use the lessons of the past to cope with the challenges of the future.

BIBLIOGRAPHY

GENERAL BOOKS

Van Emden R. and Humphries S., All Quiet on the Home Front; Headline, 2003

Taylor A.J.P., English History 1914 - 1945; Pelican, 1973

LOCAL BOOKS AND WORKS OF REFERENCE

Crawford M., Going to War - People of the Calder Valley and the First Weeks of the Great War; Hebden Bridge Local History Society, 2013

Dawson M. and Purdy I., The Gallipoli Oak; Moonraker, 2013

Edwards M., Hebden Bridge and District Roll of Honour; 2015

Fustianopolis : Hebden Bridge, the growth of a textile town; Hebden Bridge Alternative Technology Centre; 2011

Halifax Guardian Historical Almanack

Hebden Bridge Local History Archive, Eastwood Congregational Church and School: Young People's Society, Comforts Committee, Historical Album 1914 – 1920, MISC 97/M

Hornshaw T.R. & Fowler M., Calderdale War Dead, Hornshaw and Fowler, 1995

Hornshaw T.R. & Fowler M., Calderdale War Dead: Addendum, Hornshaw and Fowler, 2000

Lee J.A., Todmorden and the Great War, 1914 – 1918; Waddington and Sons, 1922

Smith J., Royd Regeneration : Mytholmroyd Commemorative Book of the Fallen; 2011

Hebden Bridge National School (Hebden Royd C. of E. Primary School); Log Books

NEWSPAPERS
Hebden Bridge Times
Hebden Bridge and District News
Todmorden Advertiser
Halifax Evening Courier